ALL THE LITTLE THINGS

ALL THE LITTLE THINGS

LISSA
SANGREE-CALABRESE

NEW DEGREE PRESS

ALL THE LITTLE THINGS

ISBN   978-1-64137-347-0 *Paperback*

978-1-64137-674-7 *Ebook*

CONTENTS

To Guga for showing me the importance of a curious heart
and to Nana Lu for teaching me the ways of the wind.

SUNRISE (OR A BEGINNING BECAUSE WE ALL START SOMEWHERE)

———

sometimes sun(s) burn kindly
sometimes heat (on hands on stems on fur)
holds tightly
cradles gently
sings the lullaby of rivers
lonely and long
the sort of homecoming your mom likes to do when you
return
all smiles and apple pies
all heat and shining

sometimes sun(s) burn blacktop
scorched and creasing
each step echoing a hot hunger, a ballad of burning
but even here there's a welcome
(a weed in the crack a sparrow's song a hawk reflected in
those high-rise windows)
refracted
a kind of human fracture
one that hurts but also holds close
life cradled here even amongst the concrete

sometimes sun(s) burn soft
behind clouds
shadowed and cold
white expanse rolling, the sky's boulder
calm and comforting
a winter blanket meant to cloak
lulling to sleep those who sing with voices full (of flowers
of light of green)
coaxing out those who watch, seeds in beaks, covered in
the warmth of winter warriors

(sometimes we smile with fire-sharpened teeth, with hands
that won't fill)

sometimes the sun is burned.

WHAT STICKS

———

Dinner was served at 7:10. Fish was on the menu and it took a long time to prepare, so they were eating late again. Darkness had fallen, the sky a kind of dull charcoal, hazy with clouds and dust. Mom would be bent over the sink, shoulders hunched, hair falling loose from her bun. She would blow the strands out of her face, use the edge of her shoulder to push loose hair behind her ear, hands too covered in fish scales to be of help.

Sometimes Lorie wondered if it was worth it, twenty minutes spent with an aching neck, all for a serving of halibut. An expense in time and money. But Dad was celebrating a promotion and Mom was celebrating the end of the workweek. Lorie thought that maybe she was supposed to be happy about something, too, maybe something with her little brother Davie's second-grade math test? She couldn't quite remember.

It took almost two hours, when it was all said and done. Twenty minutes for Mom to clean the halibut. Another hour to cook it and the rice, an extra twenty minutes to add the finishing touches and make sure the seasoning was just right.

Lorie wasn't quite sure why Mom insisted on fully preparing the fish herself, why she bought it wholesale straight from the fisherman, not even once touched by a blade. She thought it had something to do with safety, with the idea that those working in fish stores wouldn't be as careful. Lorie wasn't sure. She thought the big knives needed for gutting were cold and cruel; she would just as soon have them out of her home, safe behind storefront glass.

"Lorie, dinner's ready!" Mom had the kind of smile that was a little too wide. Her voice sounded as though she were trying to swallow something heavy. The kitchen was an artificial clean, as if it had been rubbed spotless by tired hands. As if it was in a magazine. The counter sat in the middle, neat even in its cooking mess. The dining room, through the old door at the back of the kitchen that still managed to creak despite many applications of oil, was plain but stately. All dark wood and draping tablecloths.

"Ready!" Quickly, Lorie stood, pushing herself up from the dining room table. She had already put out the good tablecloth, the one from Grandma with the white lace, and set out the plates that had seen three generations and no less than ten homes already. They were only a little chipped.

Lorie stepped into the kitchen just as Davie sprinted in, nearly colliding with the corner of the marbled counter.

"Fish?" he asked, with a slight lisp. He still had not fully shed his vocal baby fat. Lorie liked to tease him about it and on her better days, she would sit with him and read off the names of different bugs to help rid him of it. Dad had always loved insects and had passed that affection down to his children. The three of them could spend hours piled around one of their many entomological books, going through pictures and memorizing scientific names. They often quizzed each other over dinner,

"Quick, sacred dung beetle!" her dad would quip, eyes glinting,

"*Scarabaeus sacer*," Davie would shout back, his "S"s coming out a little heavy. Lorie would repeat it after him, often nudging him with her foot until he slowed down and tried it again.

Mom could never truly understand their fascination with learning the names of insects. She didn't see the point in learning what to call something that she would never see. Dad thought there was value in all knowledge. Davie liked the pictures. Lorie wasn't quite sure what she liked about the encyclopedias. She hated memorization for school, and truthfully, Davie was better at the insect names than she would ever be. She enjoyed turning the pages of the old book, each one holding a new organism. There was something about seeing all that life, all that beauty, all in one place, all for her.

Sometimes, Lorie liked to imagine she could feel tiny feet crawling on her, hear the thrum of iridescent wings. Sometimes, she could almost hear it, so close she was surprised when Davie didn't let out that barking laugh he made when the world caught him off guard.

Dad hadn't quizzed them at dinner in a little over a month. He came home from work more tired than before, less indulgent. Mom seemed to be a bit quieter too, as if she was a bit farther away.

Mom cleared her throat, nodding at Davie as she answered his question. "Yes, fish, halibut." Mom pulled the tray of fish off the stove, shuffling past Lorie and out into the dining room. Lorie could hear Dad whistling some old fisherman's song as he walked down the hall. It sounded vaguely familiar, like something she had heard in a dream.

"Daddy!" Davie jumped up to cling to Dad's leg as he entered the kitchen. Davie was seven, six years younger than Lorie, and still firmly in the running-and-tackling-by-way-of-greeting phase of elementary school. Dad let out one of his big bowl-you-over laughs and stumbled past Lorie into the dining room, ruffling her hair and winking at her as he entertained Davie. Lorie smiled. Maybe fish would be worth it after all.

"Lorie, would you like to say grace?" Mom sounded a little less strained when she asked. Her hair had been let down and it fell in soft waves around her shoulders. A few stubborn wisps curled up at her temples still, stiff with sweat that had long dried. Lorie did want to say grace. Mom had stood over the fish for almost half an hour; she had a lot to be grateful for.

"Bless us, O Lord, and these, thy gifts, which we are about to receive from thy bounty. Through Christ, our Lord." Lorie cracked an eye open, she could see Davie peeking. When she caught her brother's eye, she scrunched up her forehead and widened her eyes, flaring her nostrils. Davie stuck his tongue out at her. "Amen."

"Mom, Lorie was making faces at me!" Davie whined as soon as they dropped hands. Lorie smirked, watching as her dad started to cut up the fish and dole it out onto each of their plates. There was rice already served. One lemon sat sliced neatly in a tray in the center of the table. Mom had never been able to assuage Dad of his love for lemon on fish, despite all the extra spices and seasonings she added.

"Now, how would you have known that unless you had your eyes open?"

"But—"

"And you know how we feel about that." Dad had finished with the fish and was now watching them with amusement, reaching for a slice of lemon and squeezing it over his halibut, the pulp mushing along the edges of his fingertips.

"Lorie had her eyes open too!"

Lorie caught Dad's eye and he winked, putting his lemon down on his napkin and picking up his fork. The lemon was already starting to make a little wet pool around itself. Lorie hoped the napkin was thick enough to keep it off the tablecloth.

"Well, be that as it may, you wouldn't know about it unless you had your eyes open. Your sister knows better but so do you." Mom's voice was stern, but her mouth quirked up at the edges as she looked at Davie.

Davie pouted. He had yet to figure out which fights were truly fights and which were excuses for Mom to tease them.

Lorie picked up her fork, looking down at her plate and stabbing into her halibut. She had never been one for lemon.

"Find anything good in this one, hun?" Dad asked, raising his eyebrows before bringing a small piece of fish up to his mouth on the fork. Mom looked over to him, gaze softening, a strand of thick black hair falling in front of her left eye before she brushed it away, tucking it behind her ear and picking up her fork.

"Not really, more colorful than usual, lots of blues and reds." Lorie looked down at the hunk of meat on her fork. It was hard to picture it as having once been alive, swimming, having had things in its stomach. "Yasmine from down the street told me she found part of a toothbrush in hers the other day. Just the bristles." Yasmine didn't trust the butchers to clean her fish either. Mom and Yasmine had bonded over it. That and trying to find the right recipes to please their all-American husbands' palettes and honor the food of their families. Mom's Puerto Rican; Yasmine's Mexican.

Lorie thought maybe they also just liked to talk, and talk about where to buy the best adobo and the contents of fish stomachs was still talk. Sometimes, even the expected is interesting. Lorie brought the halibut to her mouth.

"This the same Yasmine who said she found a toy car wheel in her salmon?" Dad asked, eyebrow raised. Mom nodded. Lorie bit down. "I don't know, seems like she might be having you on. Most of the time, it's just those microplastics. I mean, two finds like that in a month? Seems unlikely."

Mom frowned. Lorie started to chew. Davie pushed his fork into the fish, mashing it into a paste.

"I mean, it's in the waters, George. Is it so unlikely that the fish are eating it? I mean, we know they are. Yasmine just happens to be getting the big chunks."

Something slippery soft in Lorie's mouth made her brow crinkle as her tongue prodded at the halibut. There was something there.

"I'm just saying, you've never found anything like that, and we get fish almost as often as Yasmine; it just seems strange. Statistically, it seems unlikely."

Something was definitely on the fish; Lorie almost had it off now. Subtly, she snuck her pinky finger into her mouth, scratching at the fish in her left cheek, her small nail doing the work her tongue couldn't.

"Maybe statistically, but why would she lie? She isn't saying anything the news hasn't said. It's just talk; she's just talking."

It was almost loose. Lorie scratched again and felt something detach from the fish. Quickly, she hooked it with her pinky and pulled it past her lips.

"Lorie, what's that?" Mom looked at her, eyes squinting a bit to try to make out what Lorie was arranging in her left palm.

At first, Lorie thought it was a scale. It was clear, almost iridescent, and thin, like some kind of skin. As she smoothed it against her hand, she recognized its slide. Deceptively strong, a little too perfect.

"A piece of plastic bag." Lorie was more curious than anything else. She had never eaten a plastic bag before. It was a tiny thing, a piece of what might have been a sandwich bag or perhaps the corner of one of those bags they give out in the grocery store.

"What?" Dad asked as Mom pushed herself up from the table. Davie leaned toward her, lifting himself out of his seat as his weight shifted onto his forearms.

"It can't be. I cleaned it myself." Mom took Lorie's hand and ran her fingertips over the bit of plastic that lay in her palm. She frowned. "I cleaned it myself."

Lorie shrugged, letting Davie pull at her wrist to get a better look, quickly releasing her again once he realized that there wasn't much to see beyond a piece of spit-covered clear bag. It wasn't much bigger than Lorie's fingernail.

"It's all right, mistakes happen. I'm sure it just got stuck to the insides of the fish while you were cleaning it, probably stuck better because of the moisture. It's such a small piece, anyway, wouldn't have caused much harm either way. It's fine." Dad handed Lorie his napkin, the one with the lemon juice on it, and Lorie carefully wiped the plastic onto it, taking care to avoid the moisture.

"I guess you're right. I'm so sorry, sweetie." Mom leaned down and gave Lorie a hug, briefly pausing to run a hand up and down her back. "Just be a little careful while eating the rest, yeah?" Lorie nodded. "That goes for you too, little man."

Davie sat back in his seat. "I'm not little."

Lorie looked down at the halibut. She thought of her dad's words. She thought of the way the plastic had stuck to the meat, as if it belonged there. It wouldn't have done her much harm if she had swallowed it. That little chunk with a little plastic on it.

She wondered how many little pieces she had accidentally eaten already. She could see the pieces building, arranging themselves into walls, blocking off her other food. She thought of the halibut. It too had only eaten a little, opened its mouth and let the small pieces in. Those small pieces formed walls in the halibut too, kept it hungry, eating, swallowing, building up what was already inside. Lorie's stomach felt like a halibut, heavy and full and empty all at once.

Lorie didn't finish dinner.

WHAT STAYS

———

There's a certain kind of silence, the type that feels a peculiar sort of full, like a cradle. It makes you understand what it is to be a mountain, to possess that kind of vast expanse, that kind of beautiful emptiness. A quiet with a kind of calm to it, like a crackling fire, or a lonely wind, or the kind of hug you give someone who is about to get on a long plane ride going far away from you. Something is being lost but in a way that isn't quite as sad as it is tearful.

That kind of silence, the type that sits quiet and sweet and calm, fills you up even as it picks at you. That kind of silence is rather hard to find. Especially when you look for it.

The kind of quiet that made Ingrid feel full hit most often after breakfast on Saturdays when the weather started to warm and the sun shone through the clouds. On those days, against the will of her mother, and to the rumbling barked protests of Muninn, she would slip out of the house, just warming up in the morning sun.

Where she lived, the wind liked to whip, and if she wasn't careful her hat, the new one her aunt had just knit her, would wind up tangled in the barbed wire fence that kept the sheep from roaming too far. She would slip out and wander down the road, take the back path, the one that cut around the slice of mountain that stood not far from their farm and across their neighbor's land.

Enok was a sweet man, and he never seemed to mind when he caught sight of Ingrid roaming on the far side of his fields, right where the flat land gave way to steep mountain. The wind was always strongest there, against the rock, the hard surface funneling the breath of the not-too-distant sea up against the cruel stone that stood, tall and patient, a silent watcher.

Ingrid liked the walks, liked greeting Enok's horses, liked "baa-ing" of the sheep as they passed her. She even liked the way the wind nipped at her clothes, trying to weasel its way against her as if it couldn't be close enough. As if by finding its way inside, it could finally get warm. Ingrid liked the walks, but she liked where she ended up even more.

Something about Icelandic silence, about the way it came over you… Ingrid didn't think it was the same anywhere else in the world. She couldn't imagine the vast cold—the sprawling life, the way the earth looked as though it had been shaped by playing giants, each one building for themselves a private world—existing anywhere else. She thought maybe the Sahara was close. It had that kind of openness, the feeling that the ground would continue forever, that the world would never stop. Maybe. She wasn't sure about the quiet there though; it seemed like it might hiss.

For Ingrid, the silence of Iceland was like no other, and it was never better than on those Saturday mornings, right after breakfast. She would walk. Sometimes motor-bike. On rare times, she would borrow the old car her mom had bought years ago, the one that puttered and took turns a little slow but kept out the wind and didn't slip. Those times, she wanted to go a bit farther, wanted to reach the water, or lose herself in the black expanse of sand.

Most of the time, however, Ingrid walked. There was something jarring about driving, even biking at times because the ground would change so fast. One second it was a flat field, the next a river, the next a mountain, the next a web of small hills. When she walked, it was slower. It seemed that sometimes she could stand right on the precipice, right at the point where two landscapes met. There, she felt a little like God. Like all of creation rolled out from her.

By far the best place to get that robust type of silence she so craved was the green fields. They didn't have a real name, nothing as significant and immediately recognizable as black sand, mountain, tundra, or forest. Green fields were what her mother always called them. Her mother would get a smile on her face when she mentioned them, one of those private ones that meant she wasn't trying to show she was happy, or make you laugh, or anything. Even after some forty-odd years of living in Iceland, even after gray hairs started to join her brown and her smile lines began to deepen, she never lost that look. She would probably have it till the day she died. She said the green fields made her that old kind of religious, meaning the kind of religious that was now called myth. She said if she stood there for long enough, seeing only nature around her, she could feel the Earth humming, the cold like the hand of some strong power clutching at her bones. Ingrid never felt anything like that. She felt the silence. She supposed that was kind of godly.

The fields weren't really anything like fields at all, nothing so flat, nothing so simple. They were bumpy, hills made entirely from rocks, forming small valleys and peaks and new odd formations seeming at once very alive and very still. And everything, every nook and almost every cranny, was covered in a vibrant green. A moss that clung and blanketed and hung off every stone. It made the ground feel alien, made Ingrid feel like she was an invader somewhere foreign. It resembled both a dystopian field, one marred by nuclear waste and the kinds of chemicals that made everything a sickly sort of vibrant, like a space in nature carved by the hand of a beautiful god.

A path had been created long before Ingrid was old enough for these walks, one that ran through the green fields, the ground rocky and strewn with pebbles, far enough from the road that you couldn't see the cars as they whizzed past, couldn't hear the rush of rubber on concrete. Ingrid had to be careful to stay on the path. She had learned that when she was young and liked to wander, when the world was a playground and she knew no danger or remorse. Her mother had scolded her, yelled her name, cried for her to come back, to watch where she stepped. Ingrid remembered feeling afraid, thinking that she might slip. Maybe some untold danger lay beneath the waves of green, beneath the old rocks. Her mother had gathered her back up and shepherded her onto the path.

Then, she had asked Ingrid to look. "Do you see?"

Ingrid had frowned, sniffed, and shook her head. She didn't see what had made her mother so sad, made the corners of her lips point down so wretchedly.

"Look closer." She pointed and turned Ingrid gently to where she had just romped so carelessly. Amidst the green there was brown. It was faint, only touching here and there, among some of Ingrid's footprints, but there it was, displayed for all the world to see.

"The moss here is fragile. When you walk on it, the moss feels it. See how your footprints are still there? See how it's not as green now? See how a little bit of you stayed out there? Now think, what if some other little girl saw you playing out there and thought to join you, think of how the moss would cry then, how it would bend to the two of you, how it would die. Now, what if there were a hundred little girls, what if even more, what then?"

Ingrid started to sniffle. She could imagine it, the way the moss would fade, vibrant green slipping into a sickly brown, how the rocks would emerge, pointed and sharp, how the green fields would change into something more sinister, more lonely.

"Do you see? Do you understand?" Ingrid started to cry, not the kind of crying she did when she was hurt, or when she wanted her mother to hug her, stop scolding, or tell her everything would be all right. This was a new, altogether unknown, type of crying.

"Oh, Ingrid." Her mother had pulled her closer, pushed her hair behind her ears, and tucked Ingrid securely against her chest. "Darling, you're on sacred land, let it love you as you love it."

Ingrid had nodded, and her mother had smiled and squeezed her tighter. Neither of them wiped Ingrid's tears; something about them felt holy.

Ever since that day, Ingrid always stayed on the path, even if it didn't always take her where she wanted it to, even when it was harder than if she just took a shorter route. Sometimes, she would see the odd footprint, a spot of brown moss in the shape of some human mark. It always filled her with a sort of profound sadness. That kind of green, that kind of beauty, took years, decades, to perfect and in the blink of an eye, in the careless step of a shoe, it could all be obliterated. Snatched up like so many stones. It was unfair. It reminded Ingrid of cruelty, of so many thefts, man's highway robberies.

Ingrid wondered what the Vikings had thought of this place, of Iceland. It was an odd place to call home, with its cold and its Martian terrain and months of darkness. What made them stop here? Of course, she knew the history—taxes and freedom and independence and all that—but what of the earth, what of the way the ground met their boots, of the way the ice called to them? The water was cold in Iceland, melting from glaciers, lapping against shores as it made its way to the arctic; the winters were colder. What made this place a home? Ingrid liked to think it was because of the silence, of the beauty that accompanied it. A Viking could think here, really ponder life. They could think of their next hunt, the best tool to carve, or the way the gods would reach into their lives and shake them until they bled. They could listen and hear nothing.

Ingrid sat down, crossing her legs and hunching over slightly, bringing her hands to her lap to protect against the cold. She sighed. She sat on a peak of sorts, one of the highest points on the little man-made path. From up here, she could see for miles and all around her the blanket of green stretched out, uninterrupted and so very alive, like she was witnessing some important secret, some sacred rite. Maybe she did understand why her mother was reminded of the Norse gods. Perhaps it had to do with the way the rest of the world seemed to sink away. Ingrid knew she wasn't alone, wasn't isolated, wasn't truly afloat in an endless sprawl of a green and rocky sea. Behind her was a mountain range, and just beyond that, one of Iceland's many glaciers, even now melting and creaking and glistening. Wasn't that wonderful, that all of that existed at the tips of her fingers, that even as she sat and let the silence consume her, there existed a whole other world not far away?

Her mother had once told her that Iceland was growing, that the land was still rising out of the sea, that by the time she had grandkids there would be more Iceland than ever before. Ingrid had grown excited, had asked if Iceland was a special place, if it was on the back of some great mountain still rising from the depths of the sea.

Her mother had laughed, soft and delicate and just a little sad. "No, it's the ice. It's melting. All this used to be under-water, those mountains, the ones just beyond our house? Those were the cliffs at the sea. The water lapped up against them and made them so sharp, so strong. When the warmer weather came and the glaciers that covered Iceland started to melt, the land started to rise; it wasn't held down by so much weight anymore. The ice is still melting now, faster than before, more than it grows, so Iceland will grow more and the land will rise to meet the sky."

"Rise to meet the sky?"

"Mmhhh." Her mother's voice was like that of a siren, lulling but maybe a bit dangerous.

"But what about the ice? I like the ice. It's so big, so blue."

Her mother smiled like Ingrid had said something smart, like she was wise. "Sometimes when something is taken away, another thing is left in its place."

Ingrid frowned. "But what about the moss? That just goes away, nothing is left in its place." That lesson still sat fresh.

"Something is left, it just isn't what you wanted to be there." Seeing Ingrid's puzzlement, her mother bent down, kissing the top of her head, using her thumb to smooth the creases in her brow, "It's like the moss, if you don't want what's left behind, you have to work to keep what's there."

"So… I shouldn't step off the path?"

Humming, her mother shook her head, something in her eyes that Ingrid couldn't quite place. "It's more like you should listen to what the world around you is trying to say. The moss was telling you to look but not touch, the ice is telling you it's melting. In both cases, you must listen and figure out how you proceed, what path you walk on."

"What if I don't hear what I'm being told?"

"Oh, I know you don't. Aren't you always late coming back when I call?" Ingrid laughed as her mother swatted her playfully on the back of the head. "I know it is hard, but you will learn, just like you learned how to hold the sheep so they don't squirm too much when we shear them."

Ingrid had nodded, not totally convinced but willing to wait and see.

Ingrid still wasn't sure if she knew how to listen. Her mother was always good at telling when there would be rain, when the wind would be too much, where they should go to find the most fulmars nesting. Ingrid was learning. She knew what kinds of clouds to look for when she wanted to know when the rain would come, the different types of wind, where the sheep were likely to get stuck in the summer when roaming free far beyond their usual pasture. She knew not to walk on the moss.

The glaciers were melting, Iceland was rising, and now she knew that Iceland was one of the lucky places. Others were sinking. As her coastline grew, others shrank, waves lapping closer and closer to homes.

Even if the green fields would grow, even if the beaches would expand, the vastness of the land she loved growing even more so, the something left would not be enough to replace the something taken away. Not worth the smaller glaciers, the sunken shorelines, the waterlogged villages and houses, the people forced to pack their culture up with them as the sea claimed their homes.

Ingrid had read somewhere that the Maldives had something like 200 inhabited islands making up the country, that most of those were at risk of sinking. Ingrid couldn't understand that, those 200, that loss. She thought it might be like if the green fields turned brown, if her special brand of silence was lost, if what made Iceland her home was taken away. Maybe.

Moss wasn't the land people live on, silence wasn't a home, a culture, a language, a life. It wasn't as if the loss of her green fields would affect many, not nearly as much as a sinking nation. Nothing as drastic. But maybe, there was something tragic in her loss too. Maybe there was something terrible in her smaller depletion, in the loss of a landscape, the loss of something that would be almost impossible to get back, and all the smaller losses that would go along with it. All those people who would never know what they were missing, would not even really mourn the disappearance of such a divine space but nevertheless would be deprived of it, of a world made a little less rich. Ingrid thought there was something sad in that, something that made her feel hollow. It seemed like the sort of silence that would be empty, that would suck you in, would eat you whole.

Ingrid thought that that sort of silence, the sort that took from you, that sat over a land of the lost. That sort of silence was starting to become all too familiar.

WHAT SLIPS AWAY

———

The symbolic bird of the town where Jared lived was a cardinal. Not formally, of course. It wasn't as if they had a town vote and everyone collectively decided that cardinals were the bird that best represented the way of life around there. Nothing so official. Something slower, gradual. Just a few instances of cardinals being used in town promotional materials, on a few banners, nothing big.

And yet, if you were to ask anyone in Jared's town, "You all have a town animal?" Everyone would say the cardinal. Something about its red coat, the way in spring its numbers swelled so that almost every other tree had a flash of red. It was beautiful. More than that, it was ordinary. Something one saw every day on their way to work, definitely the most populous bird in town.

When the new town hall was built, they named it Cardinal Hall. The name printed in big bold letters, hanging solemnly over the front door. Someone, Jared could never remember who, had proposed the name at a town meeting, one of the few town meetings that Jared had actually gone to, and it had just seemed to click. It was the only name that felt right, like a homecoming. Jared and the other townspeople had loved it—something to unify their town, to bring beauty to a drab brick building.

Cardinals weren't something Jared paid much mind to. Sure, he smiled when he saw one alight on the tree in his front yard, or when one perched near him on a fence, bush, or pole. He loved their vibrancy and their call, the way their chirps were beautifully light and airy. Their calls lined the streets on his way to school in the spring and often he would take off his headphones, letting the songs of the birds around him keep him company. It was always a soothing way to start the day. But Jared never really paid much mind to the cardinals. They just simply were.

Jared wasn't a nature person; he had always harbored a kind of deep fear of bugs, hating the way they could crawl on him quietly, without him knowing. He had forced his dad to kill many a spider for him, forced him to squash many beetles. He was often too afraid to do it himself, an embarrassing fact he had trouble admitting but was true, nonetheless. Every time he saw a creepy crawly, his heart would stuff its way into his throat and he would shout. He tried to keep the shout as manly as possible but often it came out high pitched and just a little bit strangled. His dad always told him it was okay to be afraid of something, that fear was natural and a dislike for the things that could silently infiltrate his life was normal.

But every time his dad killed a bug for Jared, he would laugh. He would always say something to the effect of, "Oh, this little thing? This little guy couldn't hurt a fly."

And then, if it was something like a spider and Jared pointed out it very much could and would hurt a fly, his dad would say, "Well, I guess you're right. Flies weren't a great example, but you're not a fly, are you, son? Good, so you got nothing to worry about."

Jared never liked that answer, would try to point out his dad's hypocrisy, reassuring one minute, teasing the next.

"Well, Jared, there's nothing wrong with being afraid of bugs, that's true, but as long as you live under my roof, I'm gonna give you grief about it. That's just the way things are gonna be." His dad had grown up in the woods of upstate New York so he was used to bugs, spiders, insects, beetles, flies, wasps and everything else that made Jared flinch.

When his dad had been a boy in grade school, he used to watch the daddy long legs walk across his desk, and when he saw a particularly big one, he would pick it up and fling it at one of the other kids in his class who didn't have such an affinity for the crawlers. Screaming chaos would ensue and Jared's dad would end up with the last laugh as everyone scrambled to help the screaming student. Jared's dad always thought it was funny,

"It's not as if they were in any real danger. I mean, it was a daddy long legs, for Christ's sake, you could literally poke those things with needles and it still wouldn't attack you. A little old thing like that never hurt anyone."

Jared thought the kids in his dad's class would probably beg to differ. It was hard for him to believe that his dad had friends in school if he pulled stunts like that but apparently, he had. Every time his dad would introduce a friend from his youth, Jared would make a point to ask them if they remembered his dad's spider-flinging days. They all did. They had all been on the receiving end at least once, even if they liked spiders, and they all had memories of watching someone else get a spider tangled in their hair.

It turned out Jared's dad had gotten in trouble many times for disrupting the class with his antics. He even got sent to the principal once when he made a girl in his class, Lavern Williams, start crying after reaching up to scratch her head and pulling her hand away with a spider on it. The girl had screamed for ten minutes straight and has staunchly refused to talk to Jared's dad ever again. Jared thought that was just what his dad deserved, and good for Lavern for sticking to it. His dad just thought it was funny.

"People really don't like spiders, it's odd. They're so small and do so much for us." Jared's dad was big on all the stuff that insects could do for them.

Jared didn't really care. He valued pollination and pest control and all that, but it all seemed very distant. They didn't own a farm and Jared wasn't planning to get into farming. In fact, he had only ever been on a farm once during a sixth-grade field trip. It had been too hot, and they had been forced to ride on a bus at six in the morning. Jared hadn't liked it very much.

All that to say Jared didn't care for nature. Despite the best attempts of his school and his father, Jared thought of nature as something nice to pass through on occasion but never get too close to. Look but don't touch.

He liked the cardinal, however. Who didn't like the cardinal? What was there not to like? Cardinals were all bright reds and beautiful calls and springtime. They reminded him of home and of that particular kind of happiness you get when it's quiet out and all you can hear is bird calls, that kind of quiet that feels like peace. He liked them, but he never paid them much mind. Why should he? They were always there, a constant.

Every morning, on his way to school, Jared passed a small pond, hidden behind a small grove of trees. He hardly ever actually saw the pond on his route, not unless he stopped and detoured so he could make his way over to the water. In the spring, even when he didn't take the little detour into the underbrush, he felt its presence. In the morning, the birds would often gather around it, the insects that depended on it for sustenance making good snacks for the hungry flyers.

The spring peepers that lined the pond were always loudest at night when he made his way home from soccer practice at school. It usually ended late, and especially in the beginning of spring, Jared often ended up making his way back home after the sun had already gone down. Dusk called to the peepers, and he always heard them on his way back home, a kind of lullaby.

That spring, one late evening, when Jared was returning home, sore and aching from practice, he noticed something was amiss. He had been deep in thought about something his coach had said, the way he ran up to the goal, the way he slowed slightly when he knew he was going to attempt a shot even before he got the ball. His coach said it made him predictable, that he could always tell when Jared thought he could make a shot by how he approached the ball.

"It makes your game vulnerable. If I can notice it, so can other people. Hell, Jared, it's not as if I'm the most perceptive bastard out there. Some of these boys are ruthless."

Jared told him that he thought it was unlikely that another player would pay enough attention to him to notice exactly how his patterns of approaching the ball manifested themselves. His coach had disagreed, had made him run another ten laps.

Jared was wearing headphones, blasting some old songs that made him think of car trips with his dad, and summer, and freedom, so he hadn't noticed at first. It wasn't until he saw his street coming up in the distance, the street sign just visible, that he had realized something was different. It was almost quiet. People tended to think the country was a quiet place, too many songs about the peace that comes with the woods, but they would be wrong. There was always some sort of noise, some call, some lone song, some rustling; it was never truly silent.

Jared took off his headphones, checking to see if the bass line was just drowning out the sound of the frogs. Nothing. Well, not nothing, there was still the sound of the peepers, calling out into the night, but it was nowhere near as loud as usual. The night sounded just a little bit empty.

The next morning, as he made his way to school, Jared listened for the cardinals. They were still there. Loud. Calling out to the other cardinals, asking for a mate, declaring themselves alive.

Jared started paying attention. He started to take off his headphones on his walk home. Started to listen for the frogs. To listen for the cardinals. His dad loved his newfound interest, and when Jared asked for his help recording the peepers every night and the cardinals every morning, he readily agreed. His dad already had some recording equipment from his brief time trying to keep an audio journal.

"It's just a little too much for me all on my own and I don't know, you always seem to like this kind of stuff."

His dad's eyes lit up. "You know your old man well."

Jared thought his dad was just hoping this would mean he wouldn't ask him to kill bugs anymore.

The cardinals were consistent. They didn't waver. Every morning they were out, lining the streets, singing. Every morning, Jared and his dad could see them flitting amongst the trees, little blips of red amidst a sea of green. If anything, Jared thought that maybe they were growing in number. He was definitely seeing them more, recognizing them throughout his days. He wasn't sure if he was just noticing now or if they really were increasing.

The peepers weren't doing as well. They weren't as loud as they used to be. His dad had noticed the change immediately. He had hummed to himself and shook his head. He seemed proud that Jared had noticed first.

Jared kept thinking about the cardinals throughout the summer and the fall. He kept thinking about them as the trees started to shiver off their leaves, as frost started to settle over the dirt. He thought about them when they were on the Thanksgiving banner at his school, wings flapping open next to an overflowing cornucopia. As winter slowly started to thaw and life started to flow back into every corner, as green started to creep in around the edges, Jared found himself anticipating their return. He waited. Every morning on his walk to school, he searched the trees for flashes of red, for the reemergence of the song he had come to know so well.

When he noticed the first cardinal, he called his dad. Jared's face split with a smile, his phone full of pictures of a vague red smudge. When he showed his friends at school, they nodded, said it was cool, played along. His dad whooped when he heard. Audibly, loudly, full of the life of spring. His dad whooped, and Jared smiled brighter. They spent three hours the following weekend in the woods. They found more cardinals, each one sparking its own delight, each one its own testament to the town, to nature.

The peepers were harder to find. They took longer, were quieter. At first, Jared thought he was imagining it, that maybe he was forgetting the last spring, the volume of the frog's call. He wasn't. They compared their recordings from the last year.

They listened intently to the way the spring peepers called. They bit their lips and frowned and worried. The peepers were definitely disappearing, almost silent in their retreat. It seemed to Jared that the peepers were as synonymous with his town as the cardinal.

When he thought of spring, he thought of both red coats and night calls. He thought of a night full of life. If cardinal red was the color of the town, the call of the spring peepers was the sound. It lit up dark skies, almost as bright as stars. The peepers and their persistent noises transformed silent drives into exploratory worlds. They gave Jared, at least, a sense of peace. Their decrease made Jared feel like he was losing his home. After all, what was color without sound?

WHAT STICKS STILL

———

At first, Lorie thought nothing of it, or more accurately, tried to think nothing of it. Who cared anyway? Just a tiny piece of plastic. She accidentally bit into plastic plenty, wrappers stuck in her mouth, stickers left on fruit. It happened. It wasn't as if she had choked. And yet, it stuck with her. She found herself avoiding fish, even in its most processed nugget form. It started to make her skin crawl. She couldn't help the feeling that she was biting into something slick, something that would stick to her. The memory of the way the bag had felt in her mouth, the way it fused itself to her cheek, felt all too fresh. As though it were still there.

She avoided the fish store near her school, taking more convoluted routes on the way home in order to circumvent having to see the unblinking eyes of the dead staring up at her as she walked. Their blank eyes all knowing, too powerful as they baked in the afternoon sun, the ice around them slowly melting. The smell alone on hot or windy days was enough.

Before long, her mother noticed her aversion, made a comment about it over lunch when Lorie had once again pushed the fish tacos to the edge of her plate, instead choosing to eat all her broccoli with a gusto that felt foreign even in the midday light.

"Something wrong? You don't seem to be eating the fish." Mom chewed a bit at her lower lip and glanced with concern at the untouched food starting to tip over the edge of Lorie's plate. Her hair fell loose against her back, and she tucked and untucked it in front of her left ear as she served Lorie more of the broccoli, her hands never fully stilling.

Lorie shrugged. "Not hungry really."

"You've got to be hungry; you didn't eat much for breakfast." It was one of those Sundays that seemed to drag and flash, slow in all the in-between places but gone before you blinked. Lorie shrugged again. Breakfast felt a long way off. She could taste plastic on her tongue. She took a sip of water then stabbed into her last piece of broccoli.

"You haven't wanted fish in a while. Not since..." Mom trailed off, swallowing.

Lorie kept her eyes on her plate so she wouldn't have to see the way her mom's hands clenched around the serving spoon. Lorie didn't want to upset her.

Davie leaned toward Lorie's plate. "I'll have it."

Lorie pushed her food toward him, watching as he maneuvered the floppy tortilla onto his plate. She imagined the fish that now lay segmented, seasoned, and askew on Davie's plate. She imagined it swimming, flying through the water, free except for a heavy stomach.

"Maybe her tastes have changed," Dad said around a mouthful of salad. He was an adult, after all, and had to watch his figure and his cholesterol. He had scoffed at Mom for even offering him her famous fish tacos. Lorie hadn't been able to tell if Dad was joking.

"Lorie's a growing girl. Sometimes that happens. I haven't noticed you eating much yucca either," he said to Lorie's bent form, not quite able to meet her eyes, "and we all know how much you used to like that. Gobbled it up almost as fast as your mother could make it." He chuckled. It hung in the air, slowly settling over the table.

Mom frowned a bit deeper, brow furrowing. Davie squirted more ketchup onto his plate. The bottle made a squelching sound, ketchup splattering out in a bright red gush. Lorie made a swirl out of the condensation left on her plate from the broccoli. Mom hummed something in response.

Lorie didn't comment either way. For some reason, she couldn't bring herself to lie but telling the truth felt like a betrayal, like she was exposing herself, admitting to something too dark to name.

Dad cleared his throat, a wet sound.

Once when Lorie was little, Dad had told her Sundays were his favorite because the two of them would often spend them together, sprawled out on the floor, books between them, sunlight warming their backs. Dad's pale arm, freckled and rough, pressed against her own light brown one, still smooth with youth. Lorie wondered if Sundays were still his favorite.

"Quick, mosquito." Dad barked, a little too loud in the small room. An easy one. Something to break the tension.

"*Anopheles.*" Davie and Lorie answered in almost perfect unison, the question so familiar that the answer felt like coming home. Dad beamed, nodding. Mom laughed, something sharp and small like a glass shattering. Lorie ate another piece of broccoli.

For a while, Lorie was angry at herself for letting a little bit of plastic bother her so much. She knew it hurt Mom that she didn't want to eat fish anymore. She knew it made her feel like she ruined something, that the work she did wasn't enough. Lorie hated that. Mom worked hard; Lorie knew that. The plastic wasn't Mom's fault. Not really. Lorie hoped her mom knew that. She had tried to tell her mom that.

She knew she needed to get over it. She was tired of taking the odd route home, of making her mom's knuckles tighten slightly when she served dinner. Her mom came from a culture of food, of love through stomachs, and although she had left some of that behind when she married Dad, who was fond of mild flavors and traditional American food, she carried her Puerto Rican ancestry in her love of cooking.

Mom told Lorie that she had only visited her Puerto Rican family a couple of times, the last one when Lorie was too young to remember, young enough that the world never looked dull. Mom had loved it, the warmth, the color, the spice. It was something she held onto like the last dredges of summer.

Lorie felt like her refusal was one more nail in the coffin, one more mark of what Mom had to give up, one more way she had to twist herself to fit.

After a month, Lorie tried to eat fish. At first, it had been fine, great even. A rich flavor had filled her mouth and she felt silly for having been so childish, so over the top in her distancing. She had started to chew in earnest, swallow, take another bite. She watched Mom brighten across the table, a subtle thing, like a flower beginning to bloom. Then it hit her, a slippery feeling against her teeth. A rolling in her stomach. She had stopped, brought her fingers to her mouth, cautious, probing. A small piece of fish came away on her fingertip, pale, a bit crushed, but fish all the same.

The next bite, Lorie swore she heard the fish squeak as she bit it. She checked but no plastic greeted her fingertips, nothing but flesh and spice. Her stomach felt heavy; her tongue sat all wrong in her mouth. She had waited till Mom was done with her plate, till she went to take the clothes from the dryer to sneak into the kitchen to throw the rest of the fish sandwich out. She hid its evidence under a few napkins.

Lorie continued her alternative path home from school. She turned down the fish she was offered at dinner the next week. She tried not to watch Mom's hands while they ate.

The trip to the beach had been the final straw, what really stuck with her. Lorie wasn't a big fan of the beach, had never really fallen in love with the way water glided over her skin, something about it made her feel sticky and a little bit off. She didn't love the way sand stuck to her either, almost desperate, like it couldn't bear to let her go. But Davie loved the beach and so did her parents; so to the beach they went. Sometimes, they gave her the option to stay home, but it was always on the days when all her friends were busy. Always on days that felt too long and too hot to be cooped up inside, watching some dumb show or killing time by sitting in front of the air conditioner and feeling hours pass in puffs of cold air. Besides, there were worse things than laying out in the sun, letting her skin turn a shade or two darker, closer to Mom's natural toasted almond color.

Usually, after an hour or two of laying around, Lorie would get up, a little sun sick and off-kilter, to take a walk. Mom made her promise to stay within eye-line of their little campout, and Dad would always call for her to join him and Davie in the water, an invitation Lorie declined almost every time. There was something nice in the way he kept asking.

It was one such afternoon, sun-soaked and long, that Lorie was strolling down the beach when she saw a tuft of what looked like caramel feathers sticking up from the dunes, just after the start of the dune grass. The feathers were like a flag in the wind, ruffled and windswept, a beacon. The sand up by the top of the dunes was hot, burning the soles of her feet in a way that wasn't wholly unpleasant but felt a little bit like fire.

It was a dead bird. Lorie wasn't sure what kind; she wasn't very good at identifying shorebirds. And even if she were, the decomposed state of the thing wouldn't have given her much to work with. Lorie could see the gleam of white bone poking up between lines of matted down feathers stuck together by sand and salt. Bending, Lorie used a shell from the small stash she had started to amass on her walk to prod a bit at the thing. The feathers did a good job of holding their shape. They were almost a soft cage and stronger than they first appeared, determined. It took some doing to start to rearrange them, to break through the top layer. In the distance, Lorie heard a car backfire.

With a rip, the feathers fell away, revealing more bone and a pen. It was slightly dirtied, a bit blackened from being swallowed, from having digestive juices lap at its sides, but otherwise, it was unharmed. There was still red ink in it, almost as if it had just been set down for a moment as if by an absent-minded professor misplacing it midway through grading papers. It seemed unreal that it could exist so completely in the stomach of some bird on a beach, far from any kitchen tables and forgotten papers.

The pen wasn't alone. It rested on a bed of lost plastics, small pieces of blue and pink, chunks of yellow, green beads, all lay scattered around it like a toxic rainbow. Lorie wondered for a moment how the bird had room for food amidst all that plastic. She felt sick. The bird had to die from something. Hunger was just as good as anything else. Lorie felt around the inside of her mouth, feeling for the piece of plastic she knew was still stuck to her cheek. The sand felt a little too hot under her feet.

Lorie dropped the shell she was holding, her makeshift shovel. The shiny fragment bounced off the matted tawny feathers and came to rest, half-buried in the sand next to the bird. The sand was starting to burn. Lorie picked up the pen, extracting it from the ribcage, barely bothering to be careful, to avoid touching the spaces where flesh rots. Lorie turned back.

Mom called out to her as she approached the towels. "Back so soon? Usually your walks are much longer." She was shielding her eyes against the glare from the sun, squinting up at Lorie. Her voice had the kind of relaxed tint it got when she let the sun soak in long enough. "What's that in your hand? Find something interesting?"

"A pen." Lorie's voice was a careless kind of blank.

"A pen?" Mom asked, lowering her hand as Lorie came to sit beside her on the bigger towel. "Where did you find a pen?"

Lorie twirled the red pen over and over between her fingers. It started to blur and, for a moment, Lorie couldn't tell if it was because of how quickly her deft fingers worked or if she had started to cry.

"A bird had it." Lorie knew she sounded distant, a little lifeless, but her stomach was rolling and she couldn't quite bring herself to care.

"Lorie! You can't just take things from birds, even if it's trash. I know you had good intentions but birds can really do some damage. What if it had bitten you or pecked you or whatever it is that birds do when they're upset?" Mom seemed a little flustered, her voice got higher, and she turned to fully face Lorie.

"It was dead; it wasn't going to bite me." Lorie paused in her twirling to click at the top of the pen. It still worked. She thought about drawing on her palm to test the ink. She wasn't sure if being in the ocean and a stomach did something to whatever it was they put in pen ink.

"Lorie! Why would you go through a dead thing? Do you know how many germs there are on dead things? Tons!" Mom was starting to sound harried.

Dad and Davie were too far away to hear them, to see the way Mom became increasingly flustered. Davie shrieked, high-pitched and short, as he dodged Dad only to be hit by a small wave. Lorie shook her head.

"Yes, there are. Now, come on, let's go rinse your hands off in the ocean." Mom said as she pulled on Lorie's elbow, tugging her to stand and starting to make her way toward the water.

"What about the pen?" Lorie let herself be pulled up, be led toward the water, but clenched her fingers a little tighter around the smooth plastic in her palm.

Mom shook her head, frowning. "We'll throw it out on our way back home."

Lorie stopped, jerking herself out of the grasp of the hand on her arm. "No! That's what happened last time and look where it ended up!" Lorie stabbed her hand clutched around the pen in the direction of the dead bird. "I might as well put it back if we do that, at least the bird is already dead." Lorie knew she was being unreasonable, that Mom hadn't been the one to feed the bird the red pen, that she was just trying to help. Lorie's feet still felt like they were burning.

For a moment, Mom examined Lorie, tilting her chin up a bit with eyes slightly squinted. They stood halfway to the shoreline, the wind whipping Mom's beach dress around her legs, pulling on Lorie's hair. Davie shrieked again. Dad laughed. Nearby a seagull called out long and low.

"All right. All right, let's just clean off your hands and then we can take the pen with us, that sound like a plan?" Mom was staring at her as if she was someone new, someone odd.

Lorie swallowed, clicked the pen. "Okay."

WHAT IS FORGOTTEN

———

Every day on her way to the bus stop on the corner of her block, Viviane passed the red maple tree. It sat in its square of dirt at the edge of the sidewalk, a piece of nature afloat in a concrete sea. It had been there ever since she could remember, a big hulking thing whose branches hung over the sidewalk, forcing her to duck slightly as she passed. It was one of the biggest trees on the block, if not, in fact, the biggest.

Its bark was the thick kind you could grab in your hand and feel its roughness imprinting on your skin. It was flaked with lichen and white paint in one spot where the odd woman from down the road, the one with too many decorations on her front steps, had spilled paint a few years back. The rain had done a good job at washing away most of it, but here and there, a few spots remained.

The trunk of the tree was so wide that Viviane could barely fit her arms around the whole thing. When she was younger, she used to strain for her fingers to touch, trying to find the best angle. Now she liked that her fingertips couldn't quite meet around the tree. It made her feel like she was touching something significant. Something real.

Viviane had always liked the tree; it was one of the few spots of color on her otherwise rather monotonous block. There was the house of the woman with too many front step decorations, all rainbow and jumbled, the gate across the street that was painted an electric blue, and the red maple tree. The tree wasn't colorful all year, of course. In the summer, its leaves faded to a pleasant green. But in the fall, the leaves turned a brilliant and stark red, almost blinding in its purity, standing strong against the dull gray-tan of the concrete. The spring was Viviane's favorite part, when the red maple bloomed, all dusty apple, flowering in bushels and welcoming in the warmth of the sun.

When she was a kid, Viviane had just called the maple "the tree." It had always been obvious as to what tree she was referring to and she hadn't known what else to say. She hadn't known what type it was, had really only vaguely understood that there were different types of trees. Of course, she had known that trees didn't look the same. Some were pines, some oaks, and she had even known that some were maples. But why exactly that mattered, she hadn't been sure. She hadn't really cared either. She knew "the tree" was different and didn't really care much beyond that.

When she was in third grade, her teacher took them on a series of science field trips around the area of the school to look at trees. She patiently told them which trees were which and some ways to tell different types of trees apart. It had been pretty simple. The group of eight-year-olds had not been capable of highly specific plant identification, and they hadn't learned how to, for example, distinguish between types of oaks. But they had learned how to tell an oak from a maple from a ginkgo from a pine. It was something, and it made Viviane care. She had attached herself to her teacher on their way back to the classroom while her friends lagged behind somewhere in the middle of the line laughing at some story Allie was telling about her older brother.

"Ms. Singh, what kind of tree has bright red leaves in the fall and red flowers in spring too?"

Ms. Singh had smiled at her, turning around briefly to scan over her class and make sure they were still following close behind her, that all her ducklings were in a row. "Well, I'm not entirely sure because I haven't seen it in person, but it sounds like it could be a red maple. That's a certain kind of maple tree. They are very pretty, really red."

Viviane nodded her head excitedly. "That sounds right! It's super red, like the reddest ever."

Ms. Singh smiled, eyes warm.

"It's at the end of my block. I pass it every day when I go to wait for the bus."

"Sounds like you're lucky to have such a nice tree so close by." Ms. Singh had a way of talking to you that made you feel like you were the only person in the world worth listening to, even when she wasn't looking at you. Viviane grinned and thanked her teacher before fading back into the line to rejoin her friends, who had moved on to talking about Allie's brother's weird friend.

That night when she went home, Viviane looked up red maples on her mom's computer, scrolling through pictures that looked just like the tree on the end of her block and smiling. It had a name now, but to her, it was still "the tree."

It became commonplace to see the tree. Like nodding at a neighbor you see on your block or seeing the person who you share your commute with on the bus every day. It was routine; it made sense. But it was still special. She still marveled at the way the leaves would change, the way the flowers bloomed, like a tree on fire. She started to keep track of it, almost subconsciously at first—the first day she saw red leaves, the first day of bloom, the first day the keys of the maple appeared in spring. She hadn't known what they were at first, just little odd things that fluttered down in pairs. But then she had learned of their fun name, that they were the key to reproduction in their own right, the wind a lock they sailed upon to open.

By the time she got to high school, Viviane had a page in one of her older notebooks that she used to keep track of the tree. It wasn't much of a chore; she had to pass the maple almost every day anyway. Making a few notes about it here or there was fun more than anything. It helped her predict when the flowers would start to break through their buds in the spring, when the air would finally be warm enough to coax them out. It was satisfying to keep track, even if her friends made fun of her, teasing her about her infatuation with the tree every now and again. Her parents, for their part, had been very supportive. They found it cute how much she seemed to care about her tree, how self-disciplined she became. They thought it a rather harmless hobby.

Because of her journal, her somewhat casual observations, and her daily routine, she noticed when things started to change. It's easy to forget the small differences over time. One year's oddness becomes the next year's baseline and slowly what's normal changes until it's something brand new, until it's a mangled and marred version of what used to be. It took a while for Viviane to notice. She took her notes and watched the ways the leaves changed and forgot about anything else.

Going away to college changed things some. She wasn't at home for the turning of the seasons; she missed a lot of the firsts. Still, she asked her mom to keep track. And she did, for the most part. Her notes weren't as precise or as consistent. She often forgot to stop by the tree on her morning commute, a minute or two of observation forgotten in a late morning rush. It meant her notes were a little less accurate, done out of a motherly sense of obligation and not out of a passion. The handwriting was messier, the dates a bit more haphazard, but only a bit.

Viviane would ask about it sometimes, would check up on the tree with her mother when she remembered during their phone calls. It was very clear in the beginning that her mother humored her and would rather skip the daily checkups. About halfway through Viviane's second year away at college, her father started to do the checks too. He filled in when Viviane's mom was too busy or forgot or was feeling particularly irritable that morning. His messy scrawl was added to the notebook on taped-in pages torn from the writing pad her father carried with him in case inspiration struck, just in case he had the idea for his next book when in line at the corner store.

Viviane was fully aware that they only kept it up in exchange for her keeping up with them. She had a tendency to forget to call if she wasn't reminded, late nights and busy days getting the best of her more often than not. Her parents reminded her to call often and, in part to get them off her back and in part to get them to keep up her notes, she had told them that they didn't need to worry about her remembering anymore if they kept up their end of the bargain. Her parents had agreed somewhat reluctantly and kept their word. Personally, Viviane thought her mom secretly liked it, that the tree was starting to grow on her.

Somewhat remarkably, they were able to keep up with the documentation throughout her whole college career, save for one fall when her mother had been away on a business trip and her dad had been too sick with the flu to leave the house reliably for a little over a week.

When Viviane returned back home after college, moving back in as she settled into her first real job post-graduation and tried to get her feet firmly under her, she was greeted by a slightly battered but up-to-date notebook. Her mom looked rather smug, proud of what she and her husband had managed to do in spite of herself. Her father had shrugged when Viviane asked him if he had liked observing the red maple at all.

"It gave me something to look out for, and it's pretty easy on the eyes." He had smiled his thoughtful smile at her, the one that reminded her of ink stains and long days spent reading.

It was because of her parents' efforts that she even noticed the change. She had grown used to the rhythms of college, the way nature bent itself around the seasons in Georgia, which was a far cry from the New England weather of her home. Her internal clock for the red maple at the end of her street wasn't as fine-tuned as it used to be. As fall approached, Viviane kept her eyes out for the tell-tale changing of the maple leaves, the way they reddened. She checked every day, sometimes accompanied by her parents, who liked to pretend they were indifferent even as they shielded their eyes from the sun so they could see the leaves at the top of the tree. It had only grown bigger in Viviane's absence, a friendly behemoth who presided over the end of the street with a kind ease.

Fall wasn't as jarring; leaves always changed on a gradient, slowly, slowly, and then suddenly all at once. It was spring when Viviane really noticed.

She had been working for a while by then, toiling away in one of the newer design firms in her area. It was a lot of work but the youth of the organization meant that there was lots of potential for promotions if she kept her nose to the grindstone for year or two. College had made her accustomed to odd hours and tedious work so it wasn't too bad. It kept her busy.

As the days started to get longer again and winter finally began to release its firm grip on the northeastern USA, Viviane's examinations of the red maple got more scrupulous as she dutifully checked on the straining buds, waiting for them to burst. It felt like it dragged on forever. Every time she felt it must finally be warm enough, a cold spell would hit them and any hopes of bursting blooms were dashed against the icy sidewalks.

Finally, one day in early spring, the flowers on the maple burst open. It was almost instantaneous; one morning there was nothing, and the next it was as if a new tree had replaced the old in the night. Almost every branch was aflame with flowers. They hadn't all fully emerged, but they had started to, their soft red lighting up the street with calm color.

She had been excited to tell her parents, calling her mom while she waited for the bus. "Mom, the maple tree bloomed! The blossoms are everywhere. You should try to see it today if you have time; it's gorgeous!"

"That's great, honey! I don't know if I'll be home before it gets dark today but I'll definitely check on it tomorrow," she chuckled. "It's not as if the flowers are going anywhere."

Viviane smiled staring at the small flowers, even though her mother couldn't see them. There was a hint of wistfulness in her mom's voice like she was missing something special. Maybe she was.

"Yeah." She shifted, changing the phone to her other ear. "It's so funny, I forgot when the trees bloom here. It's not too different from at school though."

Her mother hummed her agreement. "Sometimes, it surprises me how early they bloom, I keep expecting more winter." Viviane could hear her mother rifling around in her purse as she spoke. They had both shared a small laugh before parting with "love yous" and promises to talk at dinner. Viviane had missed the sort of easy comradery she had with her parents, and now that she had graduated, their main responsibility toward her was the business of being loving, of being there casually instead of helping her learn to be a person. They had gladly adapted to their new role as seamlessly as if nothing had changed at all.

It wasn't until Viviane went to make note of the first blooms later that night when she got home from work that her mother's words came back to her. That she even thought to pay attention to the date.

A few days doesn't seem like much, not a big deal in the scheme of things. People go a few days without eating vegetables sometimes, without showering, without taking out the trash. It's not too big of a difference. Things can be forgotten or pushed back for a few days without any big disasters.

As Viviane looked at her notes, a collection of her own neat print mixed in with her mom's blocky shorthand and her father's messy script loops, what she saw was a few days difference. Whereas before the red maple had been blooming in late April sometimes early May, they had crept forward by a few days, putting their bloom date a bit earlier in the month. It wasn't much, not more than a handful of days, and really it seemed like something that she should just put down to chance. She was very tempted to write it off as such, to record her dates and move on, but something nagged at her.

In her ninth-grade English class, she had been forced to read *Walden* in some attempt to indoctrinate them all more fully into the New Englander ethos that permeated her school. It hadn't been a particularly remarkable book, she had liked some of the others much more, and her dislike for *The Catcher in the Rye* had been the most memorable part of the class, as she had been vastly outnumbered by people who were seemingly infatuated with Holden and J.D.

Salinger both. *Walden* had been a boring book that faded to the background of her other literary exploits. Now all Viviane could remember about it was the sense of the space of the woods, the majesty of the pond, and the fact that Thoreau was regarded as one of the most influential naturalists of all time, certainly most influential in New England, forever enshrined in Massachusetts legacy.

She remembered hearing her teacher drone on about Thoreau, about how many of his journals had been archived both because of the man's influence and because of the consistent data he produced during his strolls through Walden.

"Fans and ecologists alike," her teacher had lectured, gesticulating with *Walden* clenched firmly in his right hand, a little bit of dried spit stuck in his short beard, "have worked hard to sort through the information inside his writings. He was a great man. He should inspire you all with his dedication and hard work." He seemed like a bit of a bore to Viviane, but her teacher had been right about one thing: his influence made his journals easy to find. As such, it didn't take Viviane very long to unearth just what she was looking for. It didn't take long for the nagging feeling to worsen, to become something darker.

It was earlier. The emergence of flowers on her maple was decidedly earlier than that of those that Thoreau had observed and by more than a few days. It seemed like there was a difference of a week or two, although exactness was hard when talking about variable times. Viviane felt sick.

If she had noticed this in such a short time, in less than a lifetime, in just the span of her youth, than what did that mean, really?

Some part of her was calling for her to enjoy it. She had always been a spring person, had loved the emergence of life, the return of warmth and the way the sun would press against her skin. She had always grown a bit glum at the reappearance of winter. Maybe she should be happy. These earlier flowers meant an earlier spring, meant a quicker return to what she loved. Some part of her thought that was something to celebrate, something to savor. But a deeper part of her was off-kilter, stuck somewhere between disbelief and caution.

When Viviane passed the little red flowers the next morning, staring at them as she stood, still and strong, waiting for the bus, it was with a bit of trepidation. It almost felt like she had just discovered a trap and was waiting for it to snap closed. The tree that had been her anchor to home for some time, the best part of her street, felt a little like fear.

The bus came and Viviane stepped on, quickly moving to the back and snagging a window seat. Viviane peered out the foggy glass at the maple as the bus drove away, the red fading into the distance before disappearing behind the edge of a building. The nervous feeling that had settled over Viviane the night before didn't lessen.

For the first time, she wished for winter.

WHAT IS REMEMBERED

———

Isabell hated the way the forest felt empty around her. The ways the trees creaked. It was with a kind of eerie emptiness that spoke of the dead. In the books that lined her grandmother's bookshelves, that filled every shelf to the brim, trees rustled. They moaned, they bent, they tapped at windowpanes, wind whipped them up into a frenzy. Those trees were full of life. They were green and bursting and slowly but constantly changing. Those trees meant something, were the stuff of fairytales. Germany's Black Forest was supposed to be the stuff of legends after all. Her woods were meant to entice little girls, hide secrets and many evils, lead people astray. They had personality, those trees. Isabell longed for them.

What was left of the woods around her was a sorry thing. Isabell's grandmother once told her that she hadn't been to the woods in decades, in a lifetime. That had been when they were standing in the same spot Isabell was sitting now, in the forest. It had puzzled her for a bit. How could they be in the forest close to her house, the same forest she had always known, and be so far from what her grandmother called the woods?

Her grandmother had gone into the forest with her many times throughout her childhood, leading her on walks or following or just there as a silent companion. Isabell had wondered about this as they had picked their way up the inclined plane, splotches of green finding their way amongst the brown. How were they both in the woods and not?

The forest had a way of crackling that made Isabell remember the bonfires her parents built in their yard every fall.

The state of the forest, the way it stood still, didn't particularly bother Isabell's mother, despite being grandmother's daughter. She often took walks with Isabell through the trees, taking large strides beside her, never stooping the way Gran did to look at the shoots of green poking up through the underbrush or to move aside a fallen log to look at what might be crawling beneath the surface. Isabell's mother walked through, simply held the forest at an arm's length, something pretty to look at but not really to touch, or at least, not to touch often.

When Isabell was younger, her gran had accompanied both her and her mother on their walks. Isabell, being a young child set loose, had been constantly zooming around, one minute playing in the dirt, the next crashing off ahead through fallen leaves, the next sitting by a small brook, only to repeat it all again. Her mother had watched on in amusement, never letting her eyes stray too far from Isabell's small body, vulnerable amongst the towering trees. Her gran had stopped to play in the dirt, too. She'd waited for Isabell to come crashing back toward her and stretched out a palm with a mushroom nestled safely within. She had rested by the brooks and found both the stones that had been smoothed over by generations of water and the ones that were new and sharp. She had delighted in the way Isabell rejoiced in nature. Isabell 's mother, while mostly supportive, had never fully gotten on board with their infatuation with the great outdoors.

"Mom! Watch out! Isabell's going to ruin her shirt if she keeps that up," her mother had cautioned one morning during a particularly long romp when Isabell had found a mostly decomposed log, crumbly and soft and perfect for young hands.

"Oh, she'll be fine, Christa. The shirt will clean." Gran had a way of pointing out the obvious that Isabell found endearing. Her mom often found it irritating, especially when it was in regard to topics they disagreed on.

"Of course, it will clean, Mom, that's not the point." Isabell could always tell her mom was starting to get annoyed when she clipped the end of her sentences, almost as if you could hear the period, loud and bold and daring you to challenge it.

"Oh? It wasn't?" Gran had a way of playing dumb. Isabell found that endearing too.

Over time, as Isabell got older and more capable of looking after her own shirts when she went out to play, her mother stayed at home. She never outright declined to join Gran and Isabell on their walks, but she always found something to do to keep busy, laundry, cooking, cleaning, a book that needed to be finished. Always something. Neither Isabell nor her grandmother minded much. Of course, Isabell loved her mom, loved walking through nature with her, but there was something about the way Gran could give all of herself to walking. The way she looked at the things around them, Isabell could tell she wasn't thinking about a thing except for what she saw, what she felt. There was a beauty in that, in that purity, in that connection, in that deep love. Isabell had never been able to make herself feel quite as deeply as her gran could for the natural world that was virtually in her backyard, but she spent years trying.

Isabell knew the trees weren't supposed to be brown; the branches that stood staunchly bare year-round were supposed to have leaves, something green at the very least. It was obvious; when you plant something, it grows and, almost all the time, it grows at least somewhat green. But the spruces stood bare, with only the occasional deciduous tree to break up the oppressive monoculture of shivering bark, cold and naked in the mountain air. She hadn't really thought about it too hard. That's just how the forests were, mostly brown with bits of green, splotches of brilliance amongst the monotone.

Her mother couldn't remember much different herself from her childhood, maybe a bit more greenery but not enough to really notice, certainly not enough to remember clearly. The consensus seemed to be that yes, clearly the forest wasn't supposed to look the way it did, but it did, nevertheless, and well, no one else seemed to be too worried and really it had looked like that for quite a while now, so what was the harm? The rest of the forest seemed to be doing fine after all. The Harz Mountains were still beautiful. Everyone seemed to agree, except for Gran.

It wasn't that her grandmother remembered the forest as a lush landscape where every surface blossomed with life, with a pure green, with some kind of otherworldly presence. Even she wasn't old enough for that. Gran did, however, remember what it smelled like when spring hit the woods with full force. She remembered how slowly the trees had shed their fertile leaves until their beautiful branches were only gray, a whole world wiped clean.

Gran remembered and even more than that, she read. She read old works, translations of Thoreau, the legends of the old Black Forest, and newer works, those that spoke of lush trees bathed in moonlight or the beauty of Braunlage in the spring. She read and she remembered and she longed for the woods of old. To her, the new was not the normal.

"That's how they getcha, Isabell. They convince you that what's new is what's supposed to be, that what came before is history, like it's somehow separate from the here and now. No one I know thinks of the past like that, like something old and long gone and not worth thinking about. All people do is think about the past!" Gran declared one day as they sat on a particularly large rock, the one they liked to rest at and have a snack by on hot days when the weight of the air felt like a wet towel, heavy and thick and too close.

Gran shook her head and cracked the knuckles on her right hand. It was always giving her trouble, and she had a bad habit of cracking them when she became upset about something. "These people out here act like just because they've never seen a forest full out like it's supposed to be, that it doesn't matter. That the fact they haven't seen it doesn't matter." She shook her head again. "Makes no sense."

Isabell was in the habit of listening to her gran talk without interrupting her for long stretches. She liked listening to the way Gran formed her sentences, the way she got lost in what "they" said and all the millions of reasons why "they" were wrong. Over the years, as Isabell grew older and the forest remained the same, she started to develop a furrow between her brows, started to spend more time listening to the way the wood creaked.

In gymnasium, they learned about the type of beetles that take the life right out of trees. The kind that burrow in deep and suck the soul out. The type that bore holes and open up what should be kept hidden for all the world to see. They learned about the way life, even the most stoic, can be stripped down, how it happens slowly, at an almost agonizing pace. Isabell thought that maybe the creaking was really the trees' way of crying out. It was shocking to her the number of her classmates who had sat calmly, taking notes, not the least disturbed as their teacher had laid out the start of a blight, a plague. That night, her gran had nodded along as she ranted and yelled and made herself hoarse. Gran had almost started to smile.

"Now you're starting to get it," Gran had said when it was all over and Isabell was seated, still a little hot, still unsettled. She couldn't stop hearing how the wood creaked.

The next time Isabell went into the woods, she went alone. She had to. She felt like she owed it to the trees to really listen to them, to hear if they were in fact screaming. She thought when she went back it would be different, that somehow the sounds would be new, that she would see what she hadn't before—the woods as a graveyard. But it looked the same. That was almost worse. A gravestone is a gravestone no matter how you see it, no matter what you call it. It exists regardless.

The trees, with their bald tops, their bored holes, their dry bark, stood the same. Isabell could see them now as something to mourn, as something to make her skin hot and her teeth grind. Or she could see them as she always had, the things a little farther than her backyard. That which had sheltered her, had shown her the joys of mud and the perils of slippery moss. The forest was both. It was almost worse that it was both. Isabell wasn't sure how it could be both.

One day, a dark day, Isabell told her mother she hated the forest behind their home, its deadness, its obvious lack.

Her mother had brushed her off. "You've always loved that forest, I have no doubt that whatever quarrel the two of you are having will end soon." Her mother had huffed a laugh, pleased with her own joke.

Isabell had frowned. She had been angry that her mom could think something like this could just be lived with, could be ignored. But as the week passed, so did her anger, burning out of her and leaving the hollow feeling of shame. She should still be angry. If she forgot about the woods, about the life that used to burst out of its every pore, then she was no better than all the others who had learned to move on. Who had learned to leave what was empty behind.

She tried to remember, tried to summon up the magic that had once been hidden beneath piles of leaves. She sat in the woods for hours, staring at nothing and everything all at once, trying to breathe in the life around her.

It took some doing, but it was still there, seen in the ways the wind shifted against the dead woods, in the way the roly-polies went about their business, undeterred by prying eyes or shifting ground. Isabell saw magic in the little things, but she also saw the lack of it, the spaces left behind in the wreckage. It was hard to hold both things within her at once, the good and the bad, the lovely and the devastating. It was hard to remember the past and live with the legacy of the present heavy over her shoulders.

Her gran never did end up telling her what exactly the difference was between the woods and the forest, if there ever was one. Isabell didn't need Gran to explain it anymore. She understood.

WHAT PERPETUATES

—

Malika's favorite flower was a water hyacinth. She had loved them ever since she was small. Her mother used to take her and her brothers to the lake about an hour drive from their house every other weekend. She would pack them up, amidst screams and goldfish and the chaos that came with three young children, and drive them to the lake. They went rain or shine. If Nadia decided they were going to go then they were going. Her mother had always been stubborn like that. Malika supposed that's where she got it from.

Her dad had always appreciated the time to himself. When they were younger, he had spent his evenings with them, picking the three of them up at school and shepherding them home, making dinner while simultaneously helping them with homework and making sure they didn't inadvertently destroy each other in the process.

Her mom had worked late back then, coming home around when they were getting ready for bed and seeing them off to sleep. She woke them up in the morning most days, making sure they had all safely boarded the bus before hurrying off to work. But she didn't spend much time with them during the week. Her morning encounters were full of grumpy faces, tired eyes, and lots of rushing around. The weekends though, that was her time.

Before Malika, Ali, and Abdul had gotten old enough to protest their regimented weekends, before her brothers started to spend their time playing basketball at the neighbor's, before she had started to pester her parents about sleepovers and free time; they had gone to the lake. In retrospect, Malika often had trouble remembering why they loved it so much, why the three of them had always been enthusiastic, or at least relatively so, at the hour-long trip.

When she had told her friends about the trips growing up, they always asked her what the four of them did out there. Malika could never quite recall. Somehow, it had always seemed new. She knew their trips had been filled with exploration, long walks, picnic lunches, and swimming when the weather was warm enough, but rarely remembered anything too specific. Somehow, Nadia had managed to make every visit feel exciting and new, to make the world of the lake into a new planet. It was something Malika could, and often did, look back on, some twenty-odd years later, and still feel the warmth of the sun and of her mother's smile.

One of her favorite things about the lake trips had been the plants, the way they seemed to shine in the light, their brilliance. The first time she had seen the water hyacinths, she had fallen in love with them. Their bright blotches of purple, a rather rare color in nature, shone out over the water's surface and caught her eye. Their white stood out against the water's ripples, the sun mirrored in each flower's bright yellow. They were beautiful, and she had loved the way they clumped together, a little colony on the water.

"Look, Mom! They're pretty!"

Her mother had smiled at her, indulging and loving, the way she always was in those moments. "Yes, very."

Abdul yelled something indistinct from the shoreline a few yards away, and Ali gave an answering shout.

"They're called water hyacinths." Nadia said, "They're all over."

"I like them." Malika had sat still for a few moments, eyes glued to the flowers, to the way they had crept over the water, forming a clump by the shore. Then she smiled and stood abruptly, turning to her mom. "Hi-a-sinth. I like that."

Nadia had laughed and nodded as Malika ran off to play with her brothers, floating flowers forgotten for the moment.

She had loved the flowers ever since. Their small beauty reminded her of her mother's eyes, the way the skin around them would crinkle, a kind of brilliance.

It didn't come up much, favorite flower. Sometimes it was addressed in icebreakers, as a fun fact or a "get-to-know-me" piece of trivia or something equally mundane. Hyacinths weren't the type of flower you would get a date or get someone when they graduate or perform. They weren't the kind of bouquet you bring to someone's new house to congratulate them.

So, Malika didn't see the flowers much. She had moved away from home and the childhood lake years ago and although she always meant to make time to visit the lake again, to drag her brothers and mom along with her, they had never made it out there. Malika compromised, sighing whenever she came across the odd picture of the lake.

"Yeah, it's beautiful there," she would say to friends or coworkers or whoever happened to catch a glimpse. There was always something else to do, someone else to see, some tasks that needed to be completed right then and there or it wouldn't be done at all. The lake, in all its glory, was always lost in the shuffle.

The irony that Malika finally found her way back to the lake, finally found the time, when her mother was too sick to come along, was not lost on her. She finally had time to go see this symbol of her childhood, of her family, when her family, or part of it at least, was slipping away from her. Nadia's cancer was a slow killer. Took its time meandering its way through her body, gave the family plenty of time to get back home, to say their goodbyes. She was still mostly all there, a little slower, a bit duller. But she still smiled and made you explain anything she didn't understand, still loved with a fire that blazed. Nadia was still, as always, holding herself together. It gave Malika time to return to the lake.

The irony that the flowers she loved had all but strangled the life out of the lake was not lost on her either. She stood on the edge of the lake's southern bank, where she had sat with her mother all those years ago admiring the way the yellow of the water hyacinths mirrored the sun, breath caught in her throat. In front of her, covering at least a third of the lake, lay a vast expanse of water hyacinths. They reached far out into the lake, their leaves overlapping so that Malika could hardly see the water at all. It looked like a field almost, full of flowers and leaves and nothing resembling drinkable blue.

The worst part of the whole thing wasn't even the way the lake looked as if it had shrunk, the way the flowers left their insidious mark bending the water to their will. It was that despite it all, they were still pretty. The light lavender beamed against the green, each flower a small lantern. She couldn't quite uncouple them from the flowers of her childhood, from her mother's crow's feet, now etched a little harsher into her face but no less beautiful. She still loved them despite what they had done, loved them through the goosebumps crawling over her skin.

She tried to keep her discovery to herself. She didn't want her mother to find out about what the lake had become. The idea of Nadia knowing what the flowers had done made her feel sick. But Malika had never been good at keeping secrets; it had made her an exceedingly bad confidant for her brothers, and her mother had not lost her ability to read her daughter even on her deathbed.

"Aleaziz, what's wrong? You've looked down ever since you went to the lake." Nadia sat on the couch, propped up on pillows and wrapped in one of her lighter sweaters, finding the California air a little chilly despite the sunshine.

Malika smiled at the nickname, a small one, full of something lost. She knelt next to her mother, resting her head against the armrest of the couch. Malika sighed as Nadia moved her hand to gently run her fingers through her daughter's hair.

"It was just different, kinda weird being there without you, Ali, and Abdul."

Her mother nodded but said nothing, clearly knowing there was something more and silently prompting her daughter to continue.

"And the flowers, the water hyacinths, they've taken over! The lake is almost half gone; you can barely see the water in some places. I just can't believe it."

Nadia's fingers stayed steady in her hair, gentle and warm. "I know," she said simply, no hint of surprise.

Malika sat up, catching her mother's eyes, a hint of betrayal sparking within her. "You knew? You never mentioned it to me."

Her mother nodded. "I knew it would upset you. Your father told you years ago that water hyacinths were invasive here but you said you didn't care, that they were still beautiful." Nadia shrugged. "That is true, they are. Sometimes something's beauty does not change its destructiveness, both can exist. The lake is not your responsibility. There are park management services so no use ruining something beautiful to you."

Malika frowned. She shook her head, her hands clasped tightly in her lap, nails digging a bit painfully into her palms. "No, that lake was beautiful; that lake was ours. I don't want to lose it to some flower I liked as a kid!"

Malika knew she was overreacting, but suddenly, all she could see was the way the flowers were strangling the life out of the lake. The way they were corrupting what had once been pristine. She thought of the lake as a body, as her mother's body. Suddenly, she wanted to cry, to lay down on her mother's lap and sob like she had when she was a child and the world held so many thorns.

Nadia regarded her daughter with patience, waiting for her breathing to calm, for her eyes to stop looking so misty, and then nodded. Her hand found its way back into Malika's hair. "Then don't. You can love more than one thing at once. Just because something is not the way it once was does not ruin what it is, does not mean that it has been lost."

Malika swallowed, nodded against her mother's hand. The hand was warm, surprisingly soft, old, and shaking slightly, nowhere near as steady as it had once been. Malika knew that her mother was not only talking about the lake. Like her daughter, she could feel what this conversation was about. Loss could be many things all at once. Sometimes something only half there is worse than completely gone; limbo brings its own sort of pain.

"We will always have that lake. You will always have those summers with your brothers and the flowers and me."

It was so true it hurt, a reminder that maybe a memory was all she would have. A reminder that even as she stood at the lake, it was slipping away from her, that even with her mother's hand in her hair, she was losing that gentle touch. But she could love more than one thing at once. Maybe that would have to be enough.

Warmth flooded her. She wasn't entirely sure just what she was being comforted about anymore. She wasn't entirely sure just what she was sad about anymore.

In the morning, she would go back to the lake. Maybe there was something beautiful there after all. If not, maybe there was something she could do; she had always been good with her hands.

The water hyacinth was still her favorite flower, but now maybe that wasn't so important.

WHAT STICKS ONCE MORE

———

"We eat thousands of pieces of microplastic every year." Lorie hadn't really been paying much attention to her teacher, Ms. Lewis, as she talked. Health wasn't her favorite subject but it wasn't her least favorite either. That was reserved for French. Mostly, she felt rather apathetic toward the class, maybe a bit annoyed on occasion. She found the lectures on the different types of sexually transmitted diseases and food pyramids a bit tiring and repetitive, all stuff she had heard before. But now she was listening.

"Literally thousands. Plastics are starting to invade our entire food chain, from the lowest level consumer all the way up to us, and it's not only in the packaging, it's in our food itself."

Someone in the back of the class laughed at something or other, the girl who sat two rows in front of Lorie—Samantha M.—shifted and her desk creaked. Lorie prodded at the inside of her mouth with her tongue unconsciously.

Lorie had managed to force herself to eat the fish her father had brought home the night before after claiming he forgot Lorie's newfound dislike of it. Her mother had smiled so hard she looked like she was going to burst when Lorie had forced herself to eat the small piece of a body that was put in front of her. Her father looked just a little bit relieved, his mouth softening if only for a moment. Davie had been all too happy to finish Lorie's leftovers.

The nausea that had washed over her last night returned, and Lorie felt like she was choking, as if she could feel little pieces of toy cars settling in her stomach, her throat slick with plastic bags. She reached for her water bottle. She took a sip. It helped a little. It reminded her to breathe, to swallow. Lorie tapped her pencil against her desk. She hoped the teacher had suddenly decided to start lying to the class, maybe for fun or because she was bored or as a form of retribution for them slacking off.

"I never see any plastic in my food," Samantha M. said as she raised her hand, leaning back a bit in her chair and crossing her ankles.

"Well, that's a good observation, Samantha. But you wouldn't see the pieces. They're incredibly small; that's why they're called microplastics."

Samantha raised her hand again.

"Yes?"

"Well, okay, so if they're so small then how do you know they're there at all? Seems like they might be easy to miss."

Lorie perked up. Perhaps this was when they would be told it was all some sort of cruel joke, that Ms. Lewis didn't really have any proof, that this was all meaningless conjecture.

"Some scientists who know a lot more about our trash systems than us regular folk did a study where they looked at food and water. They checked it thoroughly and repeated the process many times with many different items and in different places. This isn't a conclusion they came to lightly, which is what makes it even more important to think about."

Samantha sat back in her seat, pacified somewhat, perhaps a bit discontented at being lumped in with the "regular folk."

"Listen, everyone, I know this isn't too pleasant to think about. A lot of the things we talk about in this class can seem a bit upsetting or graphic, or generally just not something we want to be thinking about at ten o'clock in the morning. But the reality is that these things matter and exist, and when we are informed about it, we can take measures against the things that we don't like, the things we don't want to be a part of our lives."

A bit of mumbling and snickering swept over the classroom as the students made snide comments about how they should take measures against attending health, or what exactly they found unpleasant, or just that they wished it was lunch.

Ms. Lewis raised her eyebrows and flicked her eyes around the classroom, quieting the last of the murmurs. "All right, moving on…"

Lorie felt sick.

Ms. Lewis continued with the lecture; something about tap water and chemicals that Lorie wasn't fully hearing. The room seemed too bright all of a sudden. Her classmates looked varying degrees of bored, picking at hangnails, doodling, staring blankly ahead. Lorie felt as though the world was closing in around her. She felt the phantom plastics in her stomach. She remembered the toy car Yasmine had said she found in her fish. Lorie felt an engine start in her stomach, a little toy man driving his toy car to school. She could almost see him, piloting expertly around chunks of half-digested food, stomach acid acting as a great highway.

What she was thinking was absurd. Microplastics meant tiny pieces of Styrofoam, plastic bits so small she probably wouldn't notice them even if they were pointed out to her. There was no way she had swallowed a toy car. She, unlike fish, did not choose her food based on color or size. At least not most of the time. Her fear came from a deep part of herself she didn't like to think about, liked to hide away from the light. A part of her that hissed and clawed and tried to get her to doubt herself. She knew its shadow.

Still. Microplastics. Thousands. Sitting. Sitting inside her. Swallowed whole. She wondered how long they sat there, wondered if she was slowly filling to the brim like so many fish, starving herself the more she ate. Did they just stay there? Did those plastics line her stomach, some extra insulation? Did they dissolve? Did they pass on through, uninterrupted on their way to the drain? Lorie didn't know. She wondered if Ms. Lewis knew, if the scientists themselves knew. How would they? Were they in the habit of forcing people to eat microplastics and seeing if they found them again?

She brought it up at dinner. "Did you know everyone eats thousands of pieces of microplastic a year?" Lorie stared down at her plate, poking at her piece of chicken. She wondered if microplastics had made their way into birdseed yet.

"Huh, that's interesting, honey." Lorie didn't have to look up to see the strained expression that was doubtless on Mom's face. The way she bit out her vowels said enough, spoke louder than she ever would.

Dinner was often a tense affair now, a family gathering with the pretense of ease. Dad's job had gotten more stressful, Mom's attempts to help do repairs on the house in her spare time were becoming a burden that she refused to share. Lorie herself seemed to be slowly pulling away.

The only one who was ever truly relaxed was Davie. Lorie thought he was just too little to pick up on the empty way forks hit the ceramic of their dinner plates. On the way silences would stretch, thin and breakable, over the table, shushing the four of them as they ate. Sometimes, it seemed as though they were strangers.

Dad cleared his throat. Lorie poked at her chicken again.

Davie pulled a face, scrunching up his nose and looking back and forth between his plate and Lorie. "Ew, gross, is that true?" His voice held the kind of naive disgust that came with being young and gullible and dependent.

Lorie's voice still sounded like that sometimes. She wasn't sure if it was something you ever fully grew out of. There always seemed to be someone who knew more about something or other, someone who was older.

"Yes," Lorie said at the same time Dad said, "No." Dad's voice was calm, dismissive. He didn't glance up from his plate; his left hand still curled around his glass.

Lorie clenched her fork tighter in her hand and snapped her gaze up to meet Davie's. "Yes, it is, we learned about it today in health. It's real." She slid her eyes over to Dad, who looked back at her, brows raised. He didn't seem imposing then, just curious, a little taken aback maybe, not all that used to being challenged. He was the one used to doing the quizzing.

Lorie nodded. This was something she knew, something she wasn't willing to compromise on. She tried to ignore the way the inside of her mouth felt, like it was coated with something she couldn't quite place. Lorie swallowed. "It's real."

WHAT DESTROYS

—

The river had always just been. It was part of the scenery, same as cars and construction and the colors painted across brick. It was something you saw on your morning commute. Something to be commented on the same as the weather or the crazy driver you saw the other day or how your sister was doing. It just was. Sure, it flooded from time to time, summer rains keeping the river fed and plump, but usually not anything too major, nothing that called for massive renovations or reconstruction or moving.

Usually, it was fine. Usually, the Mississippi licked at its bank, hungry and just a little dangerous but relatively contained under the Missouri sun. Usually, when Tyron made his way to wherever he was going, the river was only in the back of his mind. He had assumed it would be the same this summer. That, on the way to the job he had taken to help pay for the price of life at college, the job at the snazzy new coffee shop that had opened up not too far from his house, the river would be background noise. Noticed in passing, barely spared a fleeting thought. Usually.

The summer had brought with it rain, more rain than Tyron was used to in his two decades of living not far from the river's edge. His house was about a fifteen-minute walk, about a five-minute bus ride when the traffic let up, so Tyron was used to the patterns of the river, had grown up with them practically brushing against his fingertips. It seemed like every morning brought with it a forecast for thunderstorms with no hope of a reprieve. It was hard to put a finger on why this rain felt different. Hard to say why the river crawling its way up the bank felt malicious as opposed to its usual beauty. Tyron couldn't quite explain why it struck such a chord with him.

"You've been up north too long, Pennsylvania's made you forget what it's like down here," his mother scolded him when he brought it up to her, the way the river seemed to howl. She shook a wooden spoon at him with one hand, her silver cross necklace, the one her grandma had given her when she was a girl, glinting in the light and jangling as it tapped against the buttons on her shirt. "Mississippi's always been like that. She's a cruel mistress sometimes but never too bad. Those small floods don't mean nothing."

She patted his face with her warm palm, dark as wet earth and rough from a lifetime of working in a restaurant, as she passed him. "Don't worry, boy, the rain will stop soon."

Tyron stared at his own hands, dark like his mother's but soft from months of typing on computers, of scribbling notes, of making coffees. He looked out the window, at the way the sky grayed and small droplets of rain clung to the glass like Velcro.

"Yes, Mama." She wasn't someone to argue with. She knew things deep in her bones, and Tyron had learned that his mother's bones sometimes saw things clearer than the rest of the world did. She said it was the lord's gift to her, that knowing. Tyron thought it might have something to do with the way his mother had spent a lifetime caring for those around her. But sometimes the rain felt claustrophobic, as if it was beating down on open spaces, filling them up. He could almost hear the river rushing through the kitchen.

It kept raining all week. Every morning, Tyron would trudge out the door, decked out in a light raincoat, the kind that sticks to your skin and makes you feel wet regardless, dashing to the relatively well-covered bus stop as soon as the door was shut behind him. He would spend his lunch break walking outside, letting the mist or the drizzle or the rain cover him; it was better than sitting in the storeroom in the back, cramped and too hot with the slow-revolving fan. It was better than sitting out in the cafe and looking out the window, being reminded of the corner store that had stood in that very spot only a year prior, of the way his home was starting to shift around him into something altogether unrecognizable.

On those breaks, he watched the river. The water rising was hard to notice. Nature moves slowly like that sometimes. When something builds gradually, it's harder to be afraid, of waters shifting, of stores closing. All the people Tyron talked to shrugged at him, saying it was nothing new, saying he must have forgotten what Southern storms were like when he was away at college. Saying the rent had been getting higher and higher. Saying he must have forgotten the way humidity can settle into something heavier and wetter and more permanent. That dry heat and wet heat are two different things and that you should never underestimate the ferocity of a summer storm.

He started to believe that he had just forgotten, started to let the Mississippi fade to the back of his mind, let its rumble blend in with that of the cars that lined its banks. He tried to ignore the "for rent" signs he saw throughout the neighborhood, the way some of the customers would let their eyes linger on his skin, on the waves he brushed into his hair every morning before smiling and reciting their order.

The rain kept at it, a cloudless day a seemingly rare commodity. The news warned of flash flooding but nothing too severe, some bridge closures for a few hours but no evacuation notices, nothing out of the ordinary.

Tyron watched the never-ending bustle of people in the café, buying coffee or some small treat, pulling out their laptops or their phones or meeting a friend for a drink, then shuffling off again, retreating into the humid day. He eased himself back into the kind of heat that stuck to your skin, into remembering the way rain could feel like sweat, the way the roads would steam as water evaporated in the midday sun. He remembered what it felt like to be a part of something while also being on its edges, kind of like sitting on a riverbank. He got back into the rhythm of the river, of his home, shedding his college skin, the part of him that had grown used to snow and the biting way winds can whip at you through layers of clothing. Sometimes at school, he'd felt like he could never get warm. He got comfortable in the rhythm of home.

In another few days, the rain stopped, and the sun claimed its rightful place in the sky. Only a few minor floods, nothing more than some street closures, the usual moistness that hung around in the air.

Tyron's mother teased him. "See that, boy? You had nothing to be worried about. Nothing new here, nothing changes much really, even when you're gone." She shot him a loving look, voice stern. "But that doesn't mean you get to skip out on me. Don't think just because things don't change around here, you can go skipping out on me."

Tyron hadn't been too sure about that. He wanted to ask her about the hair salon, the one that had been a few blocks away from them forever, the one that their neighbor Mariana had worked in until she had her twin boys and had to spend more time at home. He wanted to ask her if she saw the way the world was changing.

Instead, he had laughed, rocking his chair at the dinner table, balancing on its back two legs. "Don't worry, Mama, you can't get rid of me that easy."

Sometimes, he knew by the way his mom rubbed at the silver of her necklace, it wasn't about asking questions, it was about showing up. It was about sitting down at the dinner table and helping to remember what made a home so warm to begin with.

The summer was the good kind of uneventful. The kind that relaxes you, stretches itself lazily, takes its time. The cafe had an odd sort of rhythm that lulled you, pulled you into its fold. Tyron got used to it, just like he became used to a lot of things—a roommate who thought sleep was optional, the way winter numbed his toes through even his thickest socks, the way his mom sometimes looked at him as if he was something halfway gone—until he didn't even notice the click of keyboards, the hum of the big fans that circled over the store, until the "for rent" signs became something like scenery. The sounds of the river turned into the same kind of background noise it always had been, its banks and the water it enclosed forgotten.

He went away for a week. Met up with Dylan and Connor, two buddies from his floor and probably some of the closest friends he'd made at school. Dylan had commiserated with him about the cold weather and the bland food. He had told him one night when they were both a little too drunk to be bored, but too sober to lose themselves fully, that he sometimes felt that even knowing Spanish set him apart from everyone else in a way that was hard to shake, a way that meant he was always in the spotlight. Connor could be a bit thick-headed sometimes but he had known what a durag was and hadn't blinked the first time he had seen Tyron in one, which was more than could be said for some of the other boys on their floor. The three of them had become fast friends, the type that stick and stay, and Tyron was not entirely sure if he would have been able to make it through the year without them.

The three of them had decided to celebrate summer with a road trip, meeting up in Los Angeles, where Dylan lived, and driving up the west coast. Tyron had never been that far west, and Connor had never seen the desert. The three of them had been saving up before the school year had even ended, promising each other the trip was gonna work, that they were gonna find a way to inject some fun into a summer they were all otherwise spending working. Promising that their golden years weren't gone yet, that they still had a little bit of wild left in them. It felt a little surreal, taking a plane to L.A., meeting up with friends he was used to seeing on his way to breakfast, piling in a car filled with snacks and sleeping bags and just driving. A new kind of freedom—adulthood that still tasted like youth.

They hadn't had reception for a day driving through the desert, the windows down, blaring whatever songs they wanted, shouting along to them, whooping into the dusty air.

Dylan knew all the words to "Fuck Tha Police" and Connor had made a playlist of throwback songs that was so good they had already listened to it twice, hungry for the comradery it brought them—shared experiences from across cultures and the country.

With the windows rolled down, heat pummeled them. Dylan's car was a hand-me-down and the AC didn't work as well as it should so the windows stayed down, the wind as it rolled against them the only thing keeping them cool. Tyron was used to the heat; he didn't entirely mind the sweat that beaded on his forehead in the passenger seat. It was kind of exhilarating to be beyond the contact of anyone, just him and his friends and the road. It made him forget about the coffee shop's clacking keys and the river. It felt as if the three of them were all living as one.

His mom left him a voicemail. He saw it when they returned to the world of phone service and gas stations and snacks. She had promised only to call if there was an emergency, to let him have a break and forget about the responsibilities that awaited him back home, just for a little while. She had insisted on saying a prayer over him before he left, on stuffing his backpack full of snacks, of crushing his bones into her like she was trying to keep a little piece of him, but she had let him go in the end.

Connor was filling up the tank while Dylan ran to the bathroom, almost crashing into a rack of magazines in his rush, leaving Tyron in the small convenience store with a rock in his chest, pretending to browse the chip options to keep himself breathing. He clicked on the message.

"Hey, baby, turns out you were right about the river." His mom's voice came through the phone shaky and just a little bit scared. The laugh at the end of her sentence was bitter and harsh, not at all humorous. "I'm staying at your Aunt Jade's house till the water goes back down. We're all safe over here but I'm not sure how the house is doing... Look, I just called to say I love you and we're safe. We're okay. I told you I would only call in case of emergencies, and I'm trying to make good on my promise. I think this counts well enough. But—" She cut herself off and took a breath, paused. In the background of the voicemail, something heavy shifted, an audible thump reaching Tyron's ears.

Tyron wished he knew what she wanted to say, what she was holding back. She had a way of keeping things from him, like when money got tight around the time he entered high school, or when Dad had first gotten sick, or that she wasn't always as strong as she pretended to be.

"Look, have fun on your trip, sweetheart. There ain't nothing you can do here, so just... have fun. I love you." She spoke with a kind of gravity he had only heard a few times before, when things had been the kind of hard that you try to lessen in your memories. When it had been all they could do to keep from drowning. Tyron thought of bloated hands, of eyes that were a little too dull, of rushing water and creaking wood.

The message ended with a soft click, and Tyron lowered the phone from his ear. He stared at the floor, hard, and tried to keep himself from sinking, from falling face-first into the bags of snacks. He wasn't sure he would be able to stand back up again.

"Dude, they have the lime chips; those are dope!" Dylan clapped Tyron on the shoulder, all smiles and bright eyes.

Tyron nodded thoughtlessly, as though he was in a different body. All he could hear was the river roaring in his ears.

WHAT SLIPS AWAY STILL

Jared had forgotten about the fracking well. It had been installed a few years previous and was such a part of town scenery that he didn't really think of it. It was just something that was there, off in the distance, the well barely rising over the tree line when you looked just right. There had been some commotion about it initially, some town hall meetings under the watchful eye of the cardinal. But Jared hadn't really been paying attention, too caught up in the politics of recess ballgames and after-school. His dad had mentioned it a few times, some bickering in the grocery store, discontent sown amongst the tomatoes.

Jared could remember one protest. Some students and teachers had set up in front of the doors to the high school. Dressed in blue, holding signs, chanting, the whole nine yards. They had yelled something about water, something about loss, about gas staying in the ground, about the taste of chemicals on tongues. Jared hadn't fully understood.

He had told his dad about it, had mentioned that his teachers' lips tightened when he asked what it meant. His dad had said something about conflict, intersecting priorities, and Jared had nodded, already disinterested. In those days, talking to his dad was more of a chore, filled with shrugs and noncommittal grunts. Jared remembered, vaguely, the way his dad's brow had darkened. Jared had thought it was strange, maybe a bit upsetting, but generally had been more concerned with the new kid in his middle school English class.

Looking back, he could have laughed at how blasé he was, how much he missed. They built a fracking well right there, he could just make it out from the upstairs bathroom, and he hadn't really noticed. Of course, they had talked about it in class, about risk versus reward, about the way water can dirty, the way economies can boom, but really only briefly. His principal had done a good job at quieting the noise, at making sure the teachers steered away from anything the PTA would find too controversial even in science class.

It had worked. No one in his class had really paid much attention. Parents could discuss it, high schoolers who had spirit and anger and the kind of knowledge Jared found intimidating could talk about it. Not for Jared, who had a math test after lunch and didn't really know much about the chemicals that could make water toxic anyway.

There had been a big fuss originally, parents and nature lovers up in arms. But then it had faded, fallen into the background. The well had been installed. The fracking had started. The protests changed. Town hall meetings were full of complaints, full of angry voices. But then even that faded. The fracking continued. People drank the water. No one's taps caught on fire. The protesters found something else to be angry about. Those who had wanted the well felt vindicated. Everyone quieted. The town cardinal once again reigned over peace.

The water was still good, at least as far as Jared and his dad could tell. It didn't taste any different. There hadn't been a sudden rash of childhood cancer cases or anything so harsh and sudden. The taps released clean water, no amount of holding a lighter next to it resulted in an explosion or a fire. It seemed the same as it always was. But the spring peepers were quiet.

One day, during dinner, Jared's dad put his fork down, a green bean still dangling from the end, vibrating slightly. "We don't get our water from wells."

Jared blinked. His dad's eyes were bright, a little wider than normal, the kind of look he got when he figured out the way to fix something stubborn in his shop. The kind of look that made Jared feel a spark of excitement, warm and bubbling in his stomach.

"We get our water from that big watershed over east, 'bout twenty miles. We've passed it before."

Jared tried to remember, could vaguely recall a wide expanse of water. Years ago he had asked his dad if that was the ocean.

His dad had chuckled, deep and smooth, the color of honey, and shook his head. "No, that's where we get our water. Thank god, it's not an ocean or my soups would be even saltier."

Jared remembered feeling a bit embarrassed but more so impressed. He didn't know freshwater could be so vast.

Suddenly, Jared understood. They didn't get their water from the ground. It was piped in from not too far away but far enough.

"We don't drink the groundwater from around here." Jared paused, catching his dad's eye, making sure they were on the same page, "We don't drink it but we aren't the only ones here."

His dad nodded, a small rueful smile pulling at the corners of his lips. "We got a lot of small ponds in this area, lotta small springs. Lots of things that live here, most aren't too receptive to the kind of change they're getting."

Jared nodded.

His dad picked up his fork, the green bean still hanging precariously on the tip. For a moment, neither of them spoke, the excitement of the discovery fading as they sank back into the reality of what had caused their musings in the first place.

"Dad, I like the spring peepers." Jared's voice was small, smaller than he thought it would be. He couldn't take his eyes off the green bean.

"I know, son."

"They aren't cardinals; they aren't something sacred."

Jared's dad tightened his grip on the fork. The green bean tilted up. Jared chewed at his cheek.

"I know. But maybe we can make them something worth taking notice of." The green bean made its way up to his dad's lips, bitten in half with a crunch, as if to punctuate the sentence. It was as if a spell was broken.

Jared nodded, stabbing his own fork into a potato. "Maybe."

Jared had always stood out. He supposed it was a symptom of being Asian in a small town; he was destined to be noticed from the start. His dad had been the same way, one of the only kids from his hometown to be something other than cookie-cutter, something other than foggy skies. Sometimes Jared's friends, the more perceptive ones, would ask if it ever bothered him, the fact that almost no one in their small town looked like him. Jared would usually say he didn't really notice it all too much; he would usually crack some joke about not living in the Deep South or something equally non-threatening.

They meant well but Jared wasn't sure how to explain to them that even though he had never really had a big issue with anyone in town, any comments made by the more ignorant members of their school had been stopped almost as soon as they had started by a few dedicated teachers, he still noticed it. A few more glances when he walked in, looks lingering a little too long. Most of the time, it didn't bother him much.

When he stood next to his father at the next town hall and told everyone the spring peepers were disappearing, he felt the eyes anew. He had known people wouldn't take him at his word, had known that even the ones who did probably wouldn't care much. After all, it was only spring peepers, most couldn't even say what they looked like. Not too long ago, Jared wouldn't have been able to either.

He stood next to his dad and told the town hall about his many recordings, about the way he tracked the calls, about how they were diminishing. He could tell many of them were bored. They believed him then but they just didn't care. Why should they? It wasn't as if Jared had cared about the peepers for most of his life. If he had heard this information a year or two ago, he would have paid it less than no mind, if such a thing was even possible.

Jared knew that people wouldn't care, at least not till he got to the kicker. He paused, the words stuck in his throat. He didn't want to be the focus of the attention. He didn't want to be the center of the storm, didn't want to feel the way eyes would stick to him, the way people would whisper around him. He didn't want to hear the murmurs, feel the weight of people's opinions. And yet... He wanted to hear the peepers again, didn't want to feel the cold shadow of the fracking well, its icy fingers reaching out over the land and digging in.

His dad squeezed his shoulder and Jared took a breath.

"We think it's the well; it's killing them."

An uproar from the crowd, and Jared felt himself shake. His dad stood at his back, started to field questions, radiating the kind of strength that seeped into Jared's bones and propped him up. He looked out over the small crowd, angry and appalled in their orderly chairs. Over the doors, a painted cardinal flew, wings spread, beak open as if in mid-call. Jared caught its eye and sighed. Its gaze calmed him, solid and unwavering and without any judgments, only open wings and the kind of freedom that came with flight. He envied it. He felt more like a peeper, bogged down and trudging through the mud, fighting with a world set against him and trying to poison him through his skin. It was dramatic. Jared didn't care.

The hall was loud, and Jared rolled his shoulders back. The fight would be long, but maybe a few more eyes on him were worth it if he could keep those frog calls around for longer.

WHAT IS DISCOVERED

Liam's walks were mostly solitary. Most of Liam's friends thought he was odd for his morning walks, in the calm light of the sun just after it had risen, all warm and hazy around the edges. He loved the way the world yawned itself awake at 6:00 AM, flowers opening, insects just starting to hum, birds calling out their hellos. Maine mornings were crisp, even in the summer, the air nipping at his legs when he wore shorts for his excursions.

His town was small and the only others he saw out in the morning were a few of the more dedicated runners and a couple of his neighbors who had big dogs and early work times. His parents, although often awake at the time of his walks, rarely accompanied him.

Really it was for the best. Liam had started these walks about three months into his freshman year of high school.

He found they helped to clear his head of all the noise, all the demands and expectations that seemed to beat down on him, before he really had to start his day. Something about the early morning air made his thoughts solidify into something real, something he could hold onto or let go of completely.

The walks had started one morning when he couldn't sleep. His feet had been restless and his mind muddled. His mom, who had been up earlier than normal reading some book for her neighborhood book club meeting the next day, had suggested a walk. They didn't live far from the shoreline, and she thought that the ocean air might help settle him. Liam had been tired and a bit grumpy but pacing around his bedroom for an hour hadn't sounded like much fun. The hardwood floor creaked and even with the curtains drawn, it was too bright in his bedroom to feign sleep. So, he went for a walk. The next day, he went for another one. Then another.

In the beginning, he would only go a few times a week, usually not for too long. Just enough time to make it to the shoreline, skip a few rocks, and get back in time to shower and officially start his day. Then he had started to pay more attention. He had started to notice.

Liam had always known about the dead birds. It was one of those things the news mentioned every couple of months, something to be commented on in passing.

"Dead birds found on the beach, thought to be connected to recent drilling activity off the coast of Maine. More reports soon. Now, for the weather."

He could remember having conversations about it in the lunchroom, during homeroom, in some low-level biology classes where they were in the habit of giving very obvious and relatable examples of the things they taught. He was sure he had seen them on past trips to the beach with his family. He must have.

For some reason, the whole thing was rather fuzzy in his brain. He couldn't distinctly remember having noticed but couldn't remember distinctly having not noticed either, background noise. To be fair, he hadn't noticed it when his walks had first started. His direct route to the shore, his consistency, had made him a bit like a horse with blinders on, plodding the same worn path and never looking up.

One morning, about two months into his walks, he saw one. Right in front of the rock that he usually sat on was a dead bird. Liam had gotten into the habit of sitting on the rock about a month prior, finding that watching the waves for a couple of minutes did more for him than the rest of the walk altogether. It had quickly become what he looked forward to most.

In front of this rock, his rock, was a dead bird. A sandpiper, he had later discovered, a spotted sandpiper to be exact. It lay there with its white belly, covered with its trademark smattering of brown spots and thin yellow beak tipped with black, perfectly still. It jarred him. To see that bird, so close, so real, so dead. It seemed so exact. That exact rock, that exact morning, almost as if it had been placed there intentionally, as if it had been left there for him to find.

The odd thing was, at first, as Liam stood there, his sandal inches from the prone form of the sandpiper, he couldn't see what was wrong with it. It looked fine, no visible gashes or broken wings, no nearby glass windows for it to have smashed into. Perfectly healthy, except for the fact that it was dead, unmoving even as the wind pelted sand at its feathers.

He bent down, picking up one of the stones that littered the rocky beach, and poked at the small thing with the rock's tip. He peered closer, squinting and mussing up the feathers a bit with the rock's edge. It took him a comically long time to notice, to see the little flecks of oil all along the bird's feathers.

Liam had thought it was dirt, maybe small stones from being washed ashore, but it was clear when he really looked, when he actually tried to notice. The splotches of brown and black that covered large sections of the sandpiper's feathers were oil.

Odd. It didn't seem like that much. When Liam thought of birds dying because of oil, he thought of those infamous pictures of small forms covered in black, struggling to open their wings, floating atop a sea of black tar. Those birds always looked mournful, like the last dregs of nature crying out against the harsh hand of humanity, the crushing fist of industry.

Those were the pictures teachers showed when they taught about the consequences of modern industrialization.

They were what the news showed every time a new oil spill occurred. Liam thought it could be the same picture, used over and over, year after year, the news on a loop. That bird in that picture was already gone, that spill already moving out of the public consciousness even as people gasped.

Somehow, the sandpiper was different.

Such a small thing—a small bird; a small amount of oil. A small form alone on a big beach. Yet it haunted him. Liam spent ten minutes staring at it that first day. It had taken the sound of a car starting up not too far away to break him from his reverie. He had taken off his outer shirt and wrapped the small bird in it, the yellow of the fabric somehow making the fact of the oil uglier.

"Why is there a dead bird on my counter?"

Liam had taken the bird home with him that first day, had set it down on the kitchen counter, still nestled in his shirt. His mom, when she found it, at first had been disgusted, nearly throwing the body out the window when Liam was in the bathroom. He had begged her not to, had tried to explain why it was so important to him, why this bird had his heart beating fast.

"Liam, these things happen. You've seen dead things before." Her voice had been incredulous, a little frazzled, concerned.

He had. He had seen dead bugs, a dead mouse that had crawled into one of their lesser-used cabinets before taking its final breath. He had seen his great uncle too, in an open casket when he was eight, but he didn't really think that counted. That was an altogether different sort of death, something more staged, more like pretend.

Liam's mom hovered near the small bird, fingers dancing across the countertop, coming close but never quite touching the yellow shirt or what it held. Liam couldn't explain the dread in his stomach, the lead weight that had settled there that morning slowly crushing his intestines.

"Why are the two of you standing around the table with a dead bird in the center? What is that, a sandpiper?" Liam's dad hadn't understood either. They had let him keep the bird, outside the house, but still. It had sat in a small patch of grass on the left side of their door, in the shade of an old pine tree that had been there long before their family had moved in. Liam had left it there for a few days, until it started to smell.

His parents didn't complain about the scent, even though Liam caught his mom wrinkling her nose every time she was unlocking the front door. Even if the two of them didn't completely understand, they knew it was something important, something Liam was working through. Something more than a smelly sandpiper slowly rotting their front lawn.

On the fourth day, Liam had scooped up the sandpiper, still resting in the yellow shirt, which had become slightly duller over the course of the days, as if it had endured something, and had brought it with him back to the beach.

He hadn't gone back since that morning. When he started out, he hadn't been sure of why he was taking the body with him. It just felt right. The morning had been a particularly foggy one, and Liam had started to shiver a bit by the time he reached his usual rock. For a minute or two he stood, the bird and his shirt cradled in his arms, the wind tugging at his clothes, the fog settling soft and wet against his skin. He could almost imagine the bird breathing, its tiny ribcage moving up and down, its warmth heating his hands.

The bird remained dead in his arms. No longer very stiff as rigor mortis subsided. The smell was mitigated somewhat by the salty breeze coming off the water.

He had started to walk, turned and began picking his way down the rocky coastline, careful that the sandpiper remained safe, cradled close to his chest. After about twelve minutes of walking, he saw another bird on the shore. Dead. It lay belly up, its little head tilted in such a way that it seemed to be looking right at him.

Liam almost dropped the sandpiper. It wasn't the same bird. This one had a rather reddish-brown coloring to it, unlike the grayer hue of the sandpiper, but it was dead all the same. For a moment, Liam thought he was imagining it. How could he run into another one? It felt as though fate had a claw around his heart, pulling and pulling at him, refusing to let him go. He ached somewhere deep, somewhere it hurt.

Liam bent in half and scooped the new bird up in the shirt, squishing it next to the sandpiper. It, too, had a brown splotch that looked and smelled suspiciously like oil staining its stomach feathers. Liam kept walking, made his way farther down the beach, eyes searching the ground desperately.

In the end, he found three more birds. It took him two hours to return home. His parents had given him the time, worried but contained, knowing that sometimes there was a necessity in space, in grieving.

One of the birds he found that day had been newly dead, its feathers still a bit shiny-wet from the oceans lapping. The other two he found farther up the beach had already started to decay, a little putrid with a certain kind of mushiness that spoke of something halfway gone.

In the end, he had lined them up, all five in a row, emphasized against his yellow shirt, dirty and damp in the sand. He hadn't really known what to do, just felt like there had to be some record of these birds, all a bit stained, all strewn throughout the rocks, all left alone, all gone.

Liam had taken a picture. Then, carefully, he had moved the birds to just where the grass started at the edge of the beach. The birds were hidden beneath the shadow of a particularly large stone, and the distracting vibrancy of the green grasses that fought to creep their way onto the beach.

When he returned home that morning without the dead bird, Liam had almost heard the sigh of relief his parents let out, had felt the air around them sag with tension released. He showed them the picture, the birds in a row, with the seriousness of an executioner, all hard edges and regret.

"Honey." His mom had caught his eye at dinner that night, nervously fiddling with her spoon, twirling it around in one hand while her eyes remained locked on his. "This new fascination of yours, I'm not sure it's good for you."

Liam's father cleared his throat. "What we mean is, it isn't healthy for a young man like yourself to go searching these things out. These birds were once alive, and I know it may be interesting to see them this way but it is a bit troubling and it certainly doesn't seem appropriate."

Liam's mom glared at his father, who shrugged, shoulders stiff and just a little off-kilter. Liam felt a desperate laugh stick in his throat. He wondered if this was a kind of gallows humor, if maybe the yellow had been too bright a color against a dead thing.

"No, you guys don't get it. I hate that they're dead, I hate it. I didn't go looking for them that way, I just went walking; that's just what I saw. It's just what I found. I don't want to collect them or anything, I wish they weren't there at all."

Liam could tell they didn't quite believe him, could almost hear his father saying "thou dost protest too much" the way he always did when Liam fought them on something, when he stuck his neck out too fast. They had let it drop, maybe because they heard the way Liam's voice cracked, maybe recognizing this as something unwinnable, maybe because surrender is sometimes the braver choice.

The day after Liam found the five birds, his dad accompanied him on his morning walk. They didn't talk. Liam wasn't entirely sure what made him come; worry, the desire to see, the little bit of fight left in him. Liam was glad for the silence that settled between them, gentle as air.

When they got to the beach, they started to walk in the opposite direction that Liam had traveled the previous day. Liam had turned quickly when they reached the sand, walking calm and sure off to the right and his dad, wearing an old pair of loafers that were starting to come apart at the sides, had followed him wordlessly, not even bothering to reach down and take off his shoes.

It took a little while, but eventually, they stumbled on another dead sandpiper. His dad almost stepped on it as he tripped over a rock. He gasped, and Liam helped to steady him with a hand on his arm, as much reassuring as it was desperate. They both stood silent, a kind of vigil, over the body of the bird. This one had more oil on it than the others, some of its feathers coated in an unnatural black, in a death sentence.

After a while, his dad had sat, still looking down at the sandpiper. "All right Liam, all right. I think I get it now." He looked up at Liam, a frown creased deep between his eyebrows like a question mark. "Shall we put it with the others?"

After that morning, Liam had started to walk down the beach every time he arrived there. He still used it as a time to clear his head, but it was different now, more like a duty. His thoughts tended to linger on small bodies, limp and lying motionless, on the way oil seeps slow and constant, worming its way into every crack. He still used the beach to wake himself up in the morning, to make his thoughts combine, to force himself to understand. But he also searched the ground for the bodies of shorebirds, the ones no one else seemed to see, or to really notice.

Liam started to pay attention, even though it often left him a little sick after looking at those small forms laid out in rows, each one its own coffin. Still, he forced himself to notice.

WHAT DESTROYS FURTHER

There is a stillness that came with water, with abandoned homes. Pristine, like a world frozen in glass. Tyron had only ever seen high floodwaters on TV, turning neighborhoods into haunted landscapes, barren and empty with nothing left but floating boards and weeping walls. He had only ever felt the stillness through a screen, never had it lapping at his own feet, the water a dangerous mouth. It was a new world. He had returned home from his trip to discover a different home. His mother was still staying with his aunt and her family, crammed into his cousin Jasmine's room, the fifteen-year-old sleeping on the couch.

When he returned, his mother had gasped, dropping the carrot she had been peeling, bent in half over the kitchen sink, and rushed over to him. Her arms encircled him and pulled him down to her. Tyron had been taller than his mother for several years but never before had she felt small. He had always been too skinny, she always too bright, for him to see her as anything other than a giant. As Tyron held her in the kitchen of his aunt's home, he was left wondering when she had started to shrink.

"Glad you're safe, Mama," he whispered into her ear, voice a little gruffer than he intended. A little more full. "Sorry I didn't come back sooner."

She pulled back and swatted at him, gently cuffing the side of his head, her eyes soft even as she pursed her lips. "Didn't I tell ya to enjoy your trip? Ain't nothing you coulda done here anyways, God knows your aunt doesn't need you bothering her."

Tyron laughed, taking a step away from his mom and picking up his duffle bag from where he had dropped it near his shoes.

He had tried to enjoy the trip, he really had, tried to carry out his mama's wish for him as if it were a dying plea. But it was hard to let the world slide away when you weren't sure what world you had left to return to. It was hard to have fun on an aimless road trip when you weren't sure when you would be able to stop moving.

The three of them had made it to Washington, just barely making it to the airport in Seattle in time for their flights, and their goodbyes, although rushed, had been a bit more heartfelt than any of them were expecting. Connor had given him a hug full of the kind of warmth and light Tyron had thought only his mother capable of.

Dylan had looked at him straight on, his mouth quirked up at the corners in the soft kind of smile he got when he was saying something important. "There will be something there for you to come back to. It might not be what you left but it will be something that you can live with."

Tyron hadn't expected to feel so much like crying.

"Aw, come on, Ma, at least I know how to make a mean cup of coffee." Tyron shifted his duffle strap a little higher onto his shoulder and smiled, something sweet and soft.

His mother scoffed, shuffling back to the sink and picking up her carrot once more. "I should hope so, gotta get something outta watching those white people type away on their computers all day."

Tyron chuckled, shaking his head and making his way farther into his aunt's house, trying to get himself to be comfortable despite the hollow feel of his bones.

They had stayed holed up at his aunt's for another week before the waters of the Mississippi had receded enough for them to make their way back home to assess the damage. That's when Tyron noticed the stillness that permeated everything including the space between him and his mom. It even reached the neighbors the two of them encountered as they waded through the now shallow water. Everyone seemed to be silent. As if a soft rumbling quiet was radiating from their bones.

Their house felt like a stranger's. Everything was dripping and moist, the carpet in the bedrooms squished with every step. The stifling smell of wet wood was so strong it made Tyron feel sick, as if he could smell the mold forming. Pictures warped in frames. The water hadn't even reached high enough to wet them, only making it a little less than two feet off the ground, but the droplets that hung in the air corrupted far more than the flood itself had. Tyron could already see darkening spots forming on his bedsheets, mold and rot flexing their insidious fingers around their small home. They had been lucky in some ways, a lot of their more expensive items, minus the television set, had been spared, either because his mother had been able to take them with her when she evacuated or because they were in a spot that had been well enough protected from the persistent wetness.

On their trip, Dylan had told Tyron about the fires, the ones that burned down swathes of homes, the ones that licked at Californians like they were kindling. He talked about smoke in the air and flames on the news and fear on every corner. He talked about the waiting, the not knowing. Not knowing if you were going to be evacuated, if your friends were, if there would be anything left to return to when you came back looking for your home. He talked about the way nature can take, and the way the fires were worsening, the way they were growing more frequent. Dylan talked about the destruction of heat.

Looking around at his house, Tyron wasn't sure which was worse: a half-burned home or a half-submerged one. Both were unstable, both were a kind of reckoning.

Tyron surveyed his bedroom; the bedraggled sheets, the warped wood of the floors, the musty smell in the air. The white paint on his desk was peeling in strips down the side, the color cracking and splitting, dust littering the area around the desk where the paint had already been eaten away. The room felt all at once intensely his and like something he was looking at through binoculars, far away with only the appearance of being near. Tyron took a deep breath, trying to ignore the way the air settled and sagged heavy in his lungs.

He walked over to his drawers and pulled the one closest to the top open. The wood had swollen, and it took bracing his foot against the wall and several tugs for Tyron to yank the drawer free. He shook out his arm, beginning to rifle through the drawer in the hopes of finding clothes that could be saved. The advisories warned to throw away anything damp, not to risk that it could be contaminated by polluted water. Tyron knew he wasn't going to throw out everything. Most of the house had the kind of wetness that comes with still water, and it was unreasonable to think that they would get rid of their whole lives. He didn't know what they would have left at the end of this regardless.

A selfish spark in him was glad he had left so much stuff at his school, locked away in a storage facility with a few of his friends' things. He was glad for that at least, but then he remembered the way his mom's face had stiffened after they had pried the door open. He remembered the way her hands had clutched at one of the pictures of Tyron's dad that she hadn't been able to take with her, the colors bleeding, his smile all but obliterated by water. Tyron felt sick.

Redoing the electrical, refitting the kitchen, pulling up the flooring, getting rid of the mold. All of that was going to cost a lot, even with their flood insurance. There was no way that Tyron would add buying new clothes to the list of growing expenses, not if some of them could be saved with a run through his aunt's washer and dryer. Enough of their lives were washed away already.

They made two more trips back to the house, wading through less and less water, to retrieve the rest of the things they could salvage and check on the damage before construction began. They were lucky his mom had become friends with Tony, the owner and top handyman at Mendoza Housing, a few years back, and was able to get their house bumped up on the list of priorities. Tony's own house had been spared, save for the far corner of his front lawn, where his wife's flowers had gotten a bit too waterlogged for their own good, so he was anxious to help others, to help get his neighborhood back on its feet. Guilt and love were good motivators.

Tony and a few of his guys had come by their house the last time they went and walked through it. He had tried to be upbeat, keeping a kind expression on his face and delivering bad news the best way he could, assuring them that the house was fixable, that he had seen worse. Tony had given both Tyron and his mother hugs before he left, clapping Tyron firmly on the back.

"This is some crazy stuff going on, but don't worry, me and my guys got your back. You're covered." He had flashed them a smile, all yellowing teeth and sad eyes, before they had left, piling into the brown van parked out in front.

Tyron heard his mother praying that night, so desperate it sounded like sobs. For the first time in years, he thought about going to church again.

It took months for them to rebuild, for the neighborhood to get back on its feet. Tyron went back to school before it was all over, leaving his mom with promises to check-in, to come back if things got too bad. But thanks to the dedicated work of the neighborhood, of guys like Tony, of the city workers who came out in droves even when they didn't have to, their little pocket of Missouri was able to get back to some kind of working order before Tyron retreated back up to Pennsylvania.

The cafe he had worked at before the Mississippi broke her banks wasn't hit too bad, and he was able to start back up there after a month. They had been grateful for the help, given how people were scattered, and Tyron was grateful for the extra income while they tried to get their lives back together.

The river looked different to him now, now that he knew what it could do. He thought of the way it must have roared while it overflowed. Tyron's mother had told him that the water had seemed invincible, just pouring and pouring and pouring. Endless. Inevitable. She refused to walk by the river for the first two weeks, forced herself to take the long way to the grocery store, to her friends' houses. But in time, she had returned to work, or at least had returned to the restaurant to help with repairs where she could, to cook when she was able, and she had been forced to cross the river.

It got easier to cross the river without staring out at the water with a kind of concealed terror. It became easier to let the water's rushing fade in with the cars. Easier to ignore the rain when it returned, the way it made the river rise. It got easier even as they tore down the interior wall connecting the bathroom and Tyron's bedroom, even as they had to rebuild.

One evening, two months after the flood, one week before Tyron was set to return to school, he sat by the river's edge with Lena, a girl he knew from high school. She was someone familiar enough to feel comfortable sitting in silence with but strange enough to him that he kept his thoughts to himself as they looked out at the river. She lived in the flood zone herself and he knew, even as she sat there, her father and brothers were at home tearing down drywall while her mother repainted the finished rooms. Lena had only been given the night off because she had been at it all day, running errands and cleaning floors and pressing a mask over her mouth as she tore down what used to be the walls of her kitchen.

"It's funny. It looks so peaceful now, you would never know what it was responsible for, all it took." Lena didn't sound bitter, more in awe, maybe a bit tired, her bones resting heavy on the metal of the bench. Her hands, even in the dull light, looked a bit raw. A few stars poked out from behind the clouds above them. The night sky was a dark gray.

Tyron swallowed. "When I came back, at first I was paranoid, kept thinking the river was gonna flood, all that rain." He shook his head. "And then just when I got used to it, this happens. Shit's crazy." He kicked at a rock with his shoe, shifting back on the bench they were sitting on and ignoring the way it creaked beneath him.

Lena nodded, not looking over at him, her eyes transfixed on the inky waters. "And yet, it's kinda our fault in the end." She gestured around. "All this, it has consequences." Lena's eyes flicked over to him, catching his gaze as he stared at her. Lena's curly hair was pulled back away from her face, her glasses slightly askew on her nose. Her light brown skin looked paler in the odd light. "I don't know." She cracked her knuckles. "This shit's gonna happen more now, you know. Even if it's not here, it'll be happening."

The river seemed to grow louder in the background.

Tyron thought about the length of the river. The Mississippi ran long, reached far, was felt throughout the country. It meant life to millions of people, it meant livelihood. Maybe there was something beautiful in that, something sacred. Tyron thought about the "for rent" signs, about the empty buildings that lined the river, the way Dylan had been afraid that his Spanish meant that he would never truly fit in. Maybe a type of honor for where you came from made sense. Something in loving what was uncertain rang true.

Tomorrow, he had a long shift at the coffee shop. People had started to return in higher numbers, almost back to the old bustle, close enough that it was easy to pretend things were normal. So, Tyron's days were busier. He supposed he was grateful. It gave him something to do, helped him remain.

"We gotta find a way to keep going anyway. Hell, I cross that river at least once a day," Tyron retorted, not sure if he was agreeing or just reacting. He had forgotten she was majoring in geology. Not quite rivers, but close enough that to her, the earth felt sacred. That to her even something like this meant survival, meant continuing on, meant honoring the earth's literal roots. "I mean, Don't we all?"

Lena glanced at him. Her glasses seemed to glint in the dim light, like she knew some deep secret. She nodded. Tyron wanted to know what made people decide to spend their days staring at rocks.

"Exactly. We all do." Lena turned away and looked back out over the river. Tyron wondered briefly how they had gotten here, how the two of them could sit there, how they could talk about these things as if they were nothing at all, as if they were the most important thing in the world. "We all have a river. I guess we just have to keep crossing it."

Sometimes, Tyron thought that the world would be a whole lot better if people just listened to the young; they had the tendency to say something profound when no one was watching. Or maybe not. Maybe it was only possible to be this open when all the powerful adults had left the room. Tyron wasn't sure. Maybe it didn't matter.

His trip to work the next day was the same boring grind, same sitting in traffic on the bus, leaning away from the man next to him who looked like he needed the kind of rest that lasted months, same tired shuffle. He got to work early, waiting outside for his manager to get there to unlock the store. While he waited, he gazed out at the river, just visible from where he was standing. It looked so innocuous, so ordinary. Like Lena had said, peaceful, innocent. Part of him wanted to spit at it, ugly its surface. It reminded him of the way things are always changing, the way you can never go back, the way life has a tendency to pass you by.

Another part of him felt the same sort of calm love he had always had for the river; another part knew that the river was different from people, who will tear you down to replace you, to build something new from your bones. The river had a much older justice, a kind built on evolution and slowness, that felt the rush of time as much as anyone. It, too, had the world shift around it without reason. It, too, felt itself be chipped away. Maybe breaking its banks was an attempt to return, to remake.

Tyron felt the same kind of love he had for the sun, for wind, even for rain well up within him. It seemed futile to blame the river; it just ran its course, going over whatever got in its way. In this case, that meant him, his mother, Lena, the coffee shop. But all of them were nothing, as innocuous to the river as an ordinary rock, maybe even an attempt to return home.

He couldn't forgive, not entirely. It was hard to when his house was still in disarray, when his mother still anxiously waited up during rainstorms, clutching her cross and rocking, eyes closed and mouth whispering a thousand small things. But maybe it was possible. Maybe he could see past the force of the water and remember the way it brought them life. The way it rushed its way through fields and ports and pipes. Its consistency was as comforting as an old book, worn and well-read. It seemed hard, but the kind of hard that was possible.

Up the street Tyron saw his manager, Kevin, stumble out of his car, his phone gripped between his arm and his side, his hands full with keys and a water bottle, a tote bag hanging off his shoulder.

"Hey, Tyron, sorry I'm a bit late, Susie's just getting over her fever so the house is in a bit of chaos."

Tyron nodded at Kevin, thinking about how to find your home amidst what is new and stuffed his hands in his pockets. He stepped away from the cafe door as Kevin unlocked it.

The door opened and Tyron turned, letting his back face the Mississippi with a sense of calm. He could still hear the roar of the river rushing through his ears. There was a long way to go still, lots of reupholstering, lots of late nights. But he supposed he would just have to keep crossing the river, have to keep its rushing in his ears, until eventually, it felt like home once more.

WHAT STICKS
IN THE END

———

The boat ride itself was calm. The surf mild, the sun reflecting off the water. It was a perfect day.

The thin coat Lorie had brought was tied securely to her waist, her visor pulled down in a feeble attempt to keep the sun's rays from blinding her on the ride.

Off the back of the boat, being pulled along as they covered the length of the shoreline, was the newest net. It wasn't too big, didn't go down very deep. Nothing as drastic as fishermen's nets, nothing so hard to avoid. Up here, they hardly ever caught anything alive, only one or two minnows.

This net was the finest mesh they had been able to produce that could still hold up to being roughly pulled through water, that wouldn't catch so much that it split apart at the seams. It was only their second try, but so far, it looked as though it was going to get the job done. Already, from the one pass they had taken, a mound of plastic lay in one of their open containers on the deck. Satisfying, in a kind of sickening way, the product of so much time and effort, a reminder of what lay beneath the water's surface.

"It's doing good." Lorie turned, eyes sliding over the mound of plastics to land on Derek.

He smiled at her, gesturing to the net with his head. "Seems like we have got ourselves a winner here."

Lorie smiled, a small one, not quite bright enough to match Derek's. "Yeah, it might be what we've been looking for." She looked away, letting her eyes rest on the trash sitting conspicuously between them. A lot, somehow more than she had expected despite all the research, the facts and figures, the scientific studies. She knew how much was out there but seeing it, seeing the way it sat there, enough to fill the stomachs of both her and Derek several times over, made it hard for her to swallow.

"There's a lot." Lorie knew she should be celebrating, if only for science's sake. Their net was doing great and if the rest of their test runs went well, they could go forward with their proposal, work with the city, start producing the nets for sale, for implementation. They had a plan. Lorie wanted to stick to the plan; she believed in the plan. She swallowed. It felt like there was something stuck in her throat.

"I know." Derek's voice had lost its chipper edge, the optimism that he always radiated felt a bit dulled. "God, looking at all of that, just sitting there, I just—I don't know. It's just not what I expected this to feel like."

A particularly large wave splashed at the side of the boat, the spray shooting up and misting Lorie as she stood by the rail. The whole moment was a bit too much, like something fundamental had happened but no one else had noticed. The last time she had felt this way had been years ago, almost a decade now, with that tiny piece of plastic bag, the one that seemed to stick to her skin.

She remembered how disturbed she had felt, the way the earth seemed to shift around her, the way her family had gone on eating. It had been unsettling, destabilizing, had haunted her. She hadn't known what to do. Everything felt wrong, like she was trying to put a blindfold back on after seeing something horrendous. Pandora's Box was already open, no sense in trying to shut it again. But she had been young then, still subjected to her parents' whims and a bit in the background. It had taken her a while to learn that sometimes she needed to stand out. She was still learning it.

Lorie remembered her teacher had taken her aside one day, when she still hadn't been able to fully find her footing, when she was still trying to reconcile plastic bags with dinner, and had tried to set her straight.

"Look, Lorie, I know you're bright, I know you have more questions than you actually ask, but not everyone will. It's good to wait, watch, give yourself time, but you can't do it for too long. You won't always have the luxury." She had hesitated then, assessing, holding herself back a bit. Then she had sighed, looking away for a moment. "Look, sometimes people are just waiting for you to give them a reason to close the door in your face. Don't let your restraint be the reason. You have nothing to be afraid of."

Lorie had thought that wasn't exactly right. She thought of the red pen, the one that sat on her desk at home, the one she had found on the beach.

There were things to be afraid of. Plenty of things, but maybe that was kind of the point. Lorie had nodded; her teacher smiled. That night, Lorie went home and told her parents about her day. She had forced herself to look away from Mom's hands, to meet Dad's eyes the way she used to on those lazy Sundays. It had been small, but it was a start.

It had been hard at first, to find her voice, to let herself think out loud on occasion. She was used to watching. But she did it. She let words flow like water, prodded at her cheek less, felt a little less sick when she passed the fish store. Lorie had become a vegetarian, even though it made Mom twist her mouth into a frown when she thought Lorie couldn't see. Even though it made Dad regard her distantly, as if she were something to study not something to love. Davie had laughed at her. He was good like that, always had been. He was their little lighthouse, a beacon of calm amidst sometimes stormy family dinners.

Lorie remembered that time, when she was still too young to act autonomously but too old for coddling, too old for mindless orders. Maybe before the plastic, maybe before her teacher, but not after. Not then. The year she found her backbone had been the same year Dad lost his job to budget cuts and new employees and the kind of disrespect that felt like cold water in winter. It had been a hard year, full of ashy elbows and rice dinners and furrows in Mom's brow, but they had made it. Davie hadn't stopped smiling, Lorie hadn't gone silent. Dad found a new job. Mom picked up more hours at the salon. Life moved on.

Eventually, Lorie had talked herself into college, into marine biology and environmental science, and Davie had smiled his way to a psychology degree not long after—busy holding together other families now. It hadn't been an escape necessarily. Neither Lorie nor her brother had the desire to leave their parents at home, nest empty but hearts full. It had only been a step back, and although Davie—who had started to go by David, although Lorie never really called him that even now—had moved away from home so fast it made Lorie's head spin, she hadn't been so quick. She had stuck around for a bit, lingered, got back into encyclopedias of life and lazy Sundays, got into making her Mom smile and helping with dinner. She had stayed until it made sense to leave, and even then, a little longer. She stayed until it felt right.

Sometimes, as she found her way, it still felt weird, speaking her mind, stepping out not back. Sometimes, she felt out of place. But she hadn't felt like the world was tilting away from her, hadn't felt unstable the way she had with that first piece of plastic, until now.

"It's one thing thinking that there are a lot of plastics in the water, it's another seeing it." Lorie kept her eyes trained on the pile as she spoke, trying to make herself say the words that stuck in her throat. "We knew about this. Hell, we've been on other boats doing the same thing. But there's something about this pile, knowing this is ours, that's different." Out of the corner of her eye, she saw one of the metal beads in Derek's dreadlocks catch the light. She looked up abruptly. Derek's eyes remained glued on the pile.

"Did I ever tell you how I got into this work?" she asked, knowing he would shake his head before he did. "I almost ate a piece of plastic bag. It was in a fish my mom made for dinner one night and it just got stuck, a fluke thing. I think everyone thought I should get over it, that it wasn't a big deal, these things just happen. I hadn't choked. I was fine; this stuff isn't all that out of the ordinary anyway."

Derek was looking at her now, a frown wrinkling his brow.

"But that was the problem. I couldn't let it just be something ordinary." Lorie paused.

The boat's engine let out a cough and kept going. Sometimes, even now, Lorie struggled with her voice, like she wasn't entirely sure she was real. Faintly, they could hear the sound of the net trailing through the water.

"This is the same. Something ordinary. We've talked about it enough to make it so. But when you look at that pile, really look, I mean, it doesn't feel like that. It feels like something more. That's why we're here, to make it something more, to make it out of the ordinary."

Derek nodded and for a moment, the two of them just stood there. Lorie felt her jacket start to slip where it was tied around her waist.

Derek snorted, a little brightness returning to his eyes. "That may be why you are here. I'm here because you promised snacks on the boat, a promise you have yet to make good on, by the way."

Lorie chuckled, something deep and happy and maybe just a little bit free. The plastic still sat in a mound near her, and somewhere a fish was choking on a button from some kid's coat. But Lorie and Derek were on a boat with a net in the water, and Lorie was still talking, still letting the world see her and what she knew. That was something at least. It was a start.

Derek laughed, throwing a wink over his shoulder as he turned to go check on the net.

Lorie smiled. Despite the boat's rocking, the world beneath her feet felt a little more stable.

WHAT REMAINS

——

The wind that blew from the Atlantic Ocean was cold. It put a chill in his bones, always had, but Kliment took comfort in it. Out there, sitting on the small plastic chair he had dragged onto his fire escape, dirty and old and listing slightly to the left, he felt comfort against all odds.

Coney Island had the habit of looking dreary in the winter, and in the fall and just about any time of year when the sun wasn't burning. Even then, sometimes the luster of the sea, the hot shine of metal, the slow heat of the concrete would fade and settle heavy. Still, Kliment loved it there. He hadn't always. When he had first moved in, the place had been a shit hole. Still was in some ways—Coney Island was surprisingly slow to gentrify. His parents had settled in Maine when they immigrated from Russia years ago. His dad's cousin had set up shop as a lobster fisherman there and had promised Kliment's dad a job after he came to the U.S. The cousin had delivered, and Kliment had been born and they stayed.

His mom had loved it in Maine, loved the peace, the space, the way you could count all the stars. She said it reminded her of her mother's village in Russia. "There's something in the wind, Kliment, something that comforts me to my bones."

Sometimes, she had mourned the loss of her culture, of her language, the camaraderie that came from shared pasts. Kliment had caught her a few times sitting on her bed, an old shoebox open before her, staring at pictures of her home with the kind of rueful smile on her face that spoke of deep sadness but also profound love.

His dad wasn't as in love with Maine. He liked the space, thought catching lobsters was as fine an occupation as any other, and hardly ever admitted to missing his home. He didn't seem to care as much about the area around them. He was the kind of adaptable man who could be happy in a plush armchair or on a hard wooden bench. He just fit in, wherever he was put. Sometimes, he spoke of Russia with the kind of reverence reserved for a past love. Sometimes, his words were barbed and full of malice. It seemed to Kliment that his father both loathed and loved his home, the way he seemed forever at war with lobster, a food he couldn't bring himself to eat without making faces but one he depended on for his livelihood.

When he was a boy, Kliment had loved the space, the crispness of the air, the way the sun burned cold in a clear sky. Tight spaces had made his skin itch, made him miss the outdoors something fierce. When the family had made the trip down to New York to visit Sabina, an old family friend of his dad's, Kliment had gotten his first taste of city life. It had been the same year his mother got pregnant with his younger brother Ivan, the fall he turned eight.

At first, the crowded streets and towering buildings had made his skin crawl, had made him feel as though he was shrinking. But as the week wore on, Kliment had started to feel more at home. He had grown used to the noise of the city, the way it would rumble and grumble and rock him to sleep.

Two of his neighbors liked to get into screaming matches outside his borrowed window:

"I told you to turn your fucking radio down. My girl can hardly sleep!"

"Ah, fuck off, Rob. She's probably too busy with that little friend of hers to notice. I'm sure he keeps her up real late."

"What did you just say to me?!"

It seemed similar to the way the night animals would wrap their calls around him at home, like a new kind of blanket.

By the time the three—and a half—of them had left, Kliment had fallen in love. Maine felt too slow for him. He had the thrum of the city in his veins and he wanted it back. He still loved the space, the quiet, the air, the time he could spend walking with nothing around but trees, but now he missed the way pigeons would fearlessly walk behind him on the street. He liked the way nature wove itself into the cracks.

When Kliment had turned nineteen, he was more than ready to leave his small town, tired of its tininess, of the way time seemed to slow. He wanted something more. So, first chance he got, he packed up and moved to the city for college, promising to visit Ivan and his parents soon. He had moved into a tiny place in Manhattan with four other college students who were also going to NYU. The apartment was dirty and old, almost everything in it was on the brink of breaking, and he was paying too much money to live there. Still, he loved it. He loved being able to complain, comparing horror stories with friends he made at school. There was some pride in having the worst apartment or the biggest rat sighting or the strangest commute, a kind of badge of honor. But sometimes, especially at night, he would miss his home.

He missed the way his mother would laugh, all tinkling bells and sunshine, the way Ivan would run, free and fast and with the wind nipping at his heels, and he missed his dad. His steady presence, the way he could get passionate about something, quiet at first and then with such force it was almost scary, like the sea. He missed the stars, the way the Maine night seemed to extend instead of blanket. Missed the way the air pressed against his skin.

Kliment started taking photos of the way nature poked itself through the city's interior for a photography class. It started as a small assignment: just a few photos here and there of weeds poking through cement, of pigeons perched on the edge of fountains, a worm wriggling itself out of harm's way. After the assignment was submitted, he found himself wandering, still looking for ways to find little spots of the natural world amongst the city's manmade facade. He tried to find the parts of Maine he missed within the cracks and crevices of the city.

It wasn't too hard; there was a lot to see once you started to pay attention. He started taking trips to the outer boroughs more, shrugging off the taunts of his friends, their warnings not to go too deep into parts of the city that were far from safe. Manhattan liked to give itself an air of superiority that Kliment wasn't sure it entirely deserved.

It was even easier to discover the way plants liked to twist themselves around what man had made of nature a little further from the hustle of the city's center. Easier to find houses tangled with ivy, fences bisecting flowers, birds huddled together under the overpass of a subway, rattling and cold and with that certain brand of perpetual dampness. He went early, not quite brave enough to face some of the rougher areas at dusk but wanting the kind of airiness that comes from a photo taken when the sun is straddling the horizon.

Eventually, it became his routine, and even while he worked toward his degree, sat in classes and took dutiful notes about something that felt distant, he thought about where he could look next, what he could capture. His constant explorations led him to meet a man named Riley.

Riley was a photographer himself, mostly portraits, but he had started to get into cityscapes after moving to Queens. He liked Kliment's photos, said he was working on opening up a gallery, asked Kliment if he would want to be a part of it. Kliment had accepted. It had been on a whim but he liked the idea of people seeing the way in which nature could infiltrate people's lives. He liked the idea of showing people that life had a way. Something about that felt familiar, reminded him of his father's blistered hands sore from boat work, his mother's attempts to love what was foreign. It made him think of his own apartment, a little musty and small, but his home all the same.

Riley was the kind of person who didn't give up. He was a pretty large guy, bulky and big-boned with wide shoulders and a sharp Irish jaw. He was first generation like Kliment and it showed in the way he peered at the world around him. He was one to sink in his teeth, unafraid to give himself and others words of encouragement when necessary.

Those words usually consisted simply of, "Come on," but with Riley, that was often enough. Riley's voice was a little gruff, his steps long, but his hands were gentle and he had a way of smiling at people just right, a way of putting people at ease. He loved photos more than anyone Kliment had ever met and the way he would stare at each one, sometimes nodding, sometimes drumming his fingers, sometimes just looking, made Kliment feel as if he could see something beyond. If there was anyone who deserved his own gallery, it was Riley.

Kliment remembered the way the two of them had become close, working late and at odd hours, raising money by going door to door, making friends, taking photos. It had been exhausting, especially before Kliment had graduated, his schoolwork a constant nagging presence in the back of his mind. One night, one of the bad ones, when it felt like they were miles away from anything real and Kliment had a paper due in the morning, Riley had looked at him, the kind of look he usually reserved for photographs.

"Why are you doing this, Klim?" The nickname was new. The two of them had only just started to be the kind of comfortable around each other that allows for casual relaxation, moving past kind laughs to gut-busting chortles. They were both exhausted, side jobs and odd hours keeping them up late. Kliment had looked up from his papers, where he was both trying to finish a paragraph about the economic state of New York City and looking at "for rent" ads in the paper.

"Well, the paper's worth a lot of my grade and it's due tomorrow." Riley shook his head, brow a bit furrowed.

"Not what I meant." He paused, seeming to mull something over. "You got a future you know. You're bright. You don't have to spend your time with me on this pipe dream." He gestured around them to the papers piled in every available space. "You're guaranteed a space in the gallery if I ever get it up and running, I promise ya."

Kliment just stared. Something more lurked below the surface, visible in the way the light hit Riley's eyes. Kliment thought they had passed the point of tests, of seeing if the other would run, but maybe this was something new. Riley looked at Kliment as though he was expecting him to run. Maybe another man would have.

"This is as much my pipe dream now as it is yours. These photos mean something to me, too." Kliment didn't say, *You mean something to me, too.* He wasn't sure if he could just yet. Riley studied him, head cocked a bit to the side, before nodding. Kliment smiled a bit, looking back down at the papers lying before him and away from Riley's stormy eyes.

A lot remained unsaid between them. Kliment wasn't entirely sure how to voice it all. He wasn't sure how to say that sometimes the photos and Riley were all he cared about. That sometimes, Maine didn't feel real, like a hollow place far from the hustle of his life. That sometimes he felt like New York wasn't real either, that he was dreaming or hallucinating or floating away. That when he showed a friend or a neighbor or a professor his photos, there was always a moment where they were still, where they seemed to see things anew, where there was just a little bit of awe. At that moment, he felt like what he was saying was important, like he was opening the window onto a meaningful thing, although he wasn't sure just what that thing was.

They had stuck together after that night. Riley and Kliment. They opened up a small gallery. It hadn't been all that much but it had been something, and they were able to attract enough business to keep their heads above water, to stay comfortable enough. Kliment had finished school and moved to Queens to be closer to Riley and the gallery.

He had eventually moved in with Riley. The man had turned to him one night, when they were up late and sitting on the fire escape outside the kitchen window. "There is enough room in the dresser for us both, you know."

Riley blew out cigarette smoke as he spoke, only half facing Kliment, his shoulders just a little too stiff to look natural. It was more articulate than either of them tended to be about the way things were. It seemed odd to Kliment now, looking back, that the two of them had managed to tangle themselves together so completely and yet hadn't been able to voice what was on both of their lips.

Back there on the fire escape, Kliment had nodded, reached for the cigarette dangling from Riley's fingertips, intentionally letting his touch linger. "My rent is getting to be too expensive anyways."

It was far from the kind of warm comfort of a hug or the kind of gratefulness that could heat homes, but it had been enough for the two of them. Two photographers adrift in a big city and unwilling to admit that they were scared, even then, when no one else could hear.

They had moved in together and it had been nice, the best years of Kliment's life, just him and Riley and the photos they took together and apart. They threw themselves into their cameras and the gallery and each other in increasingly passionate ways, letting themselves draw strength from each other, letting themselves feel less afraid.

The city had been full of mystery, and beauty, and the kind of dull perfection that Kliment thought he had only really seen expressed in old paintings.

But then Riley had gotten sick. The kind of sick that he couldn't be cured of, the kind that ate away at him until he was nothing but skin and bones, that scarred his skin, his broad body reduced to something small. Kliment watched as the city, as the country, as his whole world fell apart, as Riley withered away like so many others had. They were careful but they were young and they hadn't always seen their bodies as something to protect. It seemed perverse to Kliment that he could sit by, fine, healthy, while the only other person who had ever really understood him, the one he shared mugs with, imploded.

Riley hadn't wanted one of the small sad funerals that seemed to pop up every other day; he had wanted photos and friends and grief held together by love. Kliment had tried to give him that, to keep his heart from breaking long enough to fill out this last wish, to keep beauty in Riley's memory. It was hard. He was tired, his friends were tired. AIDS had a way of wearing people out whether they were sick themselves or not. In the end, Kliment wasn't sure he had totally succeeded. The funeral had been small and sad, but it had also been beautiful, and although Riley's parents barely said a word, they did come. Kliment hoped it had been enough.

Kliment had stopped taking photos for a while after Riley passed. He had kept the gallery running, hiring a few more people for help, but hadn't been able to bring himself to look through a lens. The city lost its intrigue. All around him was suffering and all he could see were gaunt and haunted faces, the dull eyes of the almost-deceased.

Little flowers sprouting through concrete lost their color; fall leaves held no joy. They were as sterile as horrid hospital rooms, the ones that felt like tombs. The gray of the asphalt, the looming shadows of the skyscrapers, that was all he could see. Cold metal, hard stone, impassive trains, and rushed passersby. The city felt like it had that first time he visited so many years ago; too small and too big all at once. It gave him a kind of claustrophobia.

He visited home, stayed for longer than his typical weekend. Ivan had a family, two little girls. They loved climbing trees more than anything and were confused when their uncle Kliment, always one to point out the different types of flowers in the backyard, barely came outside. His mother fussed over him even in her old age, made him coffee and tea and soup and tried to make him smile. Even in Maine, he couldn't shake the gray off. The leaves looked dust-coated, the sky gloomy.

On his mother's suggestion, he begrudgingly started to take a walk every day.

"It'll clear your head. Make you feel better." So, she shooed him out of the house every morning after breakfast with some small suggestion of a person to go pay a visit to, or a garden that looked particularly remarkable that maybe he would like to photograph. He never took his camera. To pick one up felt like a kind of betrayal. It made him think of an empty apartment filled with things only half his.

It went on like that for a week or two, until one morning his father had off from work. Even in his old age, the man went down to the pier every day. He didn't go out catching anymore, his joints too stiff to drag up the traps, but he managed the boats, made sure shipments went to the correct people, that all the fishermen showed up on time. On some days, he still steered the boat. Kliment knew those were the days he liked best even if he had never said as much. The two of them ate breakfast together, in a silent companionship. Kliment remembered how he barely noticed his own silence in those bleak weeks, it felt as though it always clung to him.

"I showed some of your pictures to Rob from the docks. He liked them." His father kept his eyes on the newspaper he had clutched perhaps a bit too tightly in his hands.

"Hmm," Kliment hummed in response, non-committal and distant.

"No, he meant it. He's never been down there, to New York, but he said he did not think it would be like that. He did not think there was any green." Ever so slightly, his father lowered the newspaper, so his eyes were just barely visible over the top of it. "He said it gave him hope." They had been quiet after that, but something had shifted in the silence. Kliment hadn't been able to place it.

His parents had only met Riley once. They rarely visited New York; the trip was long and his dad was always anxious about leaving work, but the day the gallery opened, they had both been there. His parents had known about Riley. The two of them had been caught up in each other's lives for long enough at that point that the ripples of their involvement had reached outside their little bubble of New York City life.

Kliment's parents had been a little out of their element there, in the small gallery in an odd corner of Queens, filled to the brim with young art enthusiasts, more flamboyant members of the city, and the little old landlady who leased them the space.

Kliment's mother had once confessed to him when he was still in college that his "smart friends" made her self-conscious, made her feel just a bit stupid. It had made Kliment sad, that this smart strong beautiful woman could be made to feel small by a twenty-something who had read one paper by Freud and thought they knew something about how the world worked. So, when his parents huddled in the corner, both clutching at their glasses of cheap wine and trying to keep up, Kliment had felt like just another one of those people who passed his parents by because of the way their accented English rolled off their tongues.

Riley had gone up to them, of his own accord, without any suggestion from Kliment, without even a conversation. He knew why the two of them were uncomfortable. Of course, he did; he had listened to Kliment talk about the way his mother would shrink, the way his dad could grow so distant it was as if he weren't there at all. Riley knew and he saw and he had gone over to talk to them. He had introduced himself and gone on talking about the nearest photo to them, some black-and-white piece done by a Filipino woman who lived in Bushwick and was an absolute genius with a camera.

Riley had talked the way he always did about photography; passionately, and with such an honest appreciation that Kliment's parents had started to open up. Riley had a way of listening that made you feel smart, like what you were saying was the most important thing in the world. Kliment thought he had never thanked Riley enough for that night.

After that, his parents had asked after Riley, even talked to him a few times on the phone when the two of them had moved in together, and Kliment would call his parents on those rainy afternoons that made you cuddle up against soft chairs. Kliment may have never told them about Riley, not really told them, but he didn't think he needed to. There are some things parents know without being told. Besides, sometimes labels create more trouble than they're worth. Kliment had Riley, Riley had him, and his parents seemed happy with that. It was more than others got.

In his childhood kitchen, with his father looking at him over the top of his paper, Kliment wanted to spill it all then, to tell his father all that they were, to tell him about the way his survival felt like its own kind of loss. Instead, he said, "I miss him." It was short but it held the weight of something more.

His father nodded, resting the paper on top of the table. "I know. But the world goes on. Outside it is spring, you still have your camera, you are still you. You miss him, yes, it still hurts, yes, but outside it is green. You must remember that it is green." The words were spoken softly, without his father's usual gruffness, with the kind of care that was usually reserved for his wife. Kliment's father had gestured with his chin toward the window where the green of leaves could be seen, vibrant and light. "Go, make a picture. Remember him."

It hadn't been immediate, his resurgence, recovery. It had taken another week for him to pick up his camera. A few days more before he could bring himself to start taking photos again, before he could do anything more than clutch desperately at the small black box, lifeless until he gave the word. But once he did, something shifted. A well inside him, unused for too long, reopened, and it was all he wanted to do.

At first, his photos were bleak with a kind of unpracticed blandness, high contrast, low lighting, flat backgrounds, utterly unlike his normal work.

But he got his footing back. One day, when showing his parents the photos he had developed, his father stopped him. He looked at a picture of a small fly, momentarily resting on their old wooden doorstop. The photo wasn't technically one of his best, a bit blurry from the rushed framing, the light a little too strong so parts of the wood were washed out, but his dad had nodded. "This one is good. I like it."

His mother had agreed, and Kliment had felt himself smile. He could almost hear Riley laughing, one of his bellowing laughs, all loud and full of vibrancy.

He had returned home to New York not long after, had moved out of the place in Queens, relocating to Brooklyn for a change of scenery. The gallery was still open but it didn't need him as much anymore, and he wasn't sure if he could bear to be so close. He had missed the ocean. It gave him new inspiration. He liked its savage freedom, the way the vast beauty could seep into a city, lapping at the edges. Coney Island felt like somewhere he could grow old and grow old, he did.

Now, as he sat on the fire escape, the salt of the sea settling on his tongue, Kliment felt the kind of peace of a life well-lived, a life almost complete. Sometimes, he was struck by his smallness, the way his life was so self-contained. He had no children of his own, though plenty of nieces, and grand-nieces and nephews, to keep him happy, and he hadn't done all that much with his life. But he loved. Loved his family, his friends, his pictures, and Riley most of all. For him, that was enough. It must be.

Yes, he wished sometimes he had done more, been more of an advocate, for those who were suffering like Riley had, for the arts, for the small green things that found their way into the cruel city, but then he would remember. He would remember the way the sun hit the water just so at dawn, the way Riley had looked when he studied a photograph, the way weeds could get themselves into the oddest of places. Yes, he lived a small life, but he loved completely and as freely as he knew how. He had fought to make the world a little more beautiful, a little more whole.

The ocean would keep lapping against the shore after he was gone. Flowers would keep sprouting just where they were most needed. All he could hope for was that someone else would see the beauty of that just as he had and would love it just as much.

AUTHOR'S NOTE

———

The world is changing.

The environment is not what it once was. In some ways, that's good; no more ice sheets covering the entire globe, making life difficult. But the more the world changes, the more we change it, the more is lost. The more that is left to drift into oblivion. Some of these changes are big, ice sheets melting, disease vectors moving farther north, animals going extinct, but some are smaller, more every day.

These smaller changes can be felt locally, can be seen in earlier blooms, or an extra filter needed for water purification. They can be seen by anyone if you just know where to look, and when you start looking, you might be surprised by what you see. By the amount of knowledge and understanding that can be gained from a few extra seconds of contemplation, a few extra moments of observing.

These smaller changes, the warmer days, earlier migrations, can stay with us. While bigger issues may slip off shoulders, distance and magnitude making for an ineffective teacher, the small things tend to stick.

We remember them.

Growing up, I always cared about the environment, always considered myself a nature lover. I knew about climate issues and I cared about them, but I never really engaged with them deeply. I went to some marches, helped with trash collection and recycling in my elementary school, but never thought I would work much with the climate in the future.

In my junior year of high school, I took AP Environmental Science, mostly because of the teacher but also because I liked nature and thought the class sounded interesting. The class was, predictably, full of doom and gloom, big-picture stuff, learning about all that is wrong with the world. It was interesting, upsetting, and depressing. About halfway through the first semester, we took a trip to Prospect Park, a local Brooklyn park not too far from my own home. We were learning about water quality, and we tested the waters of a few different small ponds throughout the park. The point of the trip was to learn about the different ways that water can be polluted or affected by pollution, but one of the most powerful moments for me was seeing the algae.

Of course, I had always seen the algae that tends to blanket parts of the ponds in the spring and summer, but I had never really paid it much mind. It was pretty in a kind of disturbing way, and it seemed like it was meant to be there. Algae does grow on the top of water naturally, after all. One of the other students mentioned the algae, complaining about how it was hard to take a water sample without getting any of the small green flecks in the tube.

My teacher nodded. "That's an algal bloom, kind of gross, right?" He told us that algal blooms were a signature of pollution and climate change, enabled by fertilizer runoff and warming waters and deadly to the organisms that live in underwater. Algal blooms suck up all the oxygen and leave the water oxygen-poor, making huge dead zones devoid of life, as all the other organisms suffocate.

It seemed like such a simple thing, something so small, something that I had seen my whole life, but suddenly, it took on a new meaning. Suddenly, I was seeing just what anthropogenic change entailed firsthand. It lit something within me, something that still burns. That class, perhaps that moment, was what lead me to understand that, for me, the environment is one of the most important issues of our time, and that I had to be involved in the fight for our planet, indeed for our lives and the lives of many other organisms.

This realization, this passion, had always been within me, but it took this kind of small specialized interaction for me to see what had always been there, for me to understand that the signature of climate change and anthropogenic destruction is everywhere.

The environment definitely needs our help.

Global sea-level rise was 2.6 inches above 1993 levels in 2014,[1] storms are growing in frequency,[2] and an increase in global warming of 2°C could prove disastrous, with incredible changes to the planet, like the destruction of all coral reefs, increase of droughts and weather-related extreme events, and decreasing biodiversity as extinctions rise.[3]

These issues are frightening and large and seem overwhelming, and, unfortunately, after hearing about these things too often, people can become disenfranchised. It can feel as if there is so much to do that one person cannot possibly make an impact. Instead, people leave these issues up to those who are in the field of environmental science, those who are advocates, those who "know what they are talking about."

These big pictures issues can overwhelm and upset even the most passionate listener, and while there is value in telling people the reality of the situation, in trying to scare people into compliance, sometimes this technique can leave listeners exhausted from the sheer magnitude of the issue. These problems, especially for people who don't live in areas with immediate risks, can seem distant and scary in the way death is, dark and impending but a long way off for now.

---

1   "Is Sea Level Rising?" NOAA's National Ocean Service, October 27, 2008.

2   Ibid.

3   "Summary for Policymakers." Global Warming of 1.5°C.

This is not good. Climate change and human-caused destruction and pollution are affecting places now. It seems to me that an effective way to get people to understand this is to start small.

It can be hard to conceptualize these big-picture issues, but if we start small, start local, start personal, people can feel a connection to where they are from, to what they know. This connection can then foster action and engagement. It certainly did for me. My personal experience made me understand that the minor things matter. That for many, a connection to something visible, something local, is more powerful and more meaningful than knowledge of all possible outcomes.

It made me realize that for many people, the start of environmentalism may be in all the little things.

REFERENCES

———

WHAT STICKS/WHAT STICKS STILL/ WHAT STICKS ONCE MORE/ WHAT STICKS IN THE END

Albatross Directed by Chris Jordan. 2017.

Cox, Kieran D., Garth A. Covernton, Hailey L. Davies, John F. Dower, Francis Juanes, and Sarah E. Dudas. "Human Consumption of Microplastics." *Environmental Science & Technology* 53, no. 12 (May 2019): 7068–74.

WHAT STAYS

Worland, Justin. "Global Climate Change Effects: Iceland Land Levels Rising." *Time*, 2 Feb. 2015.

WHAT SLIPS AWAY/WHAT SLIPS AWAY STILL

Gasland Directed by Josh Fox. HBO, 2010.

Phone interview with Dr. Nancy Langston

WHAT IS FORGOTTEN

"About Phenology." Budburst.

Monahan, William B., Alyssa Rosemartin, Katharine L. Gerst, Nicholas A. Fisichelli, Toby Ault, Mark D. Schwartz, John E. Gross, and Jake F. Weltzin. "Climate Change Is Advancing Spring Onset across the U.S. National Park System." *Ecosphere* 7, no. 10 (2016).

"The Journal of Henry David Thoreau." The Walden Woods Project, September 15, 2016.

WHAT IS REMEMBERED

Arnberger, Arne, Martin Ebenberger, Ingrid E Schneider, Stuart Cottrell, Alexander C Schlueter, Eick von Ruschkowski, Robert C Venette, Stephanie A Snyder, and Paul H Gobster. "Visitor Preferences for Visual Changes in Bark Beetle-Impacted Forest Recreation Settings in the United States and Germany." Environmental management. Springer US, February 2018.

Waldmeister. "Dying Forest Syndrome in the Harz Mountains." wwwstormypicturesde, October 3, 2018.

WHAT PERPETUATES

"Water Hyacinth." National Invasive Species Information Center. Accessed August 21, 2019.

WHAT DESTROYS/WHAT DESTROYS FURTHER

"Climate Change, Extreme Precipitation and Flooding: The Latest Science (2018)." Union of Concerned Scientists. Accessed August 21, 2019.

WHAT IS DISCOVERED

Camphuysen, Kees, and Martin Heubeck. "Beached Bird Surveys in the North Sea as an Instrument to Measure Levels of Chronic Oil Pollution." *Researchgate*, 2015,

AUTHOR'S NOTE

"Global Warming and Hurricanes." GFDL.

"Summary for Policymakers." Global Warming of 1.5°C.

US Department of Commerce, and National Oceanic and Atmospheric Administration. "Is Sea Level Rising?" NOAA's National Ocean Service, October 27, 2008.

ACKNOWLEDGEMENTS

———

Writing has always seemed like a fun pastime to me but was something I figured I'd never do seriously. Even when I started out writing this book, having a finished product, something I can hold in my hands and put on a shelf, didn't feel like a reality. It has been through the journey over the past year, through all of the people who have helped me along the way, that I have been able to make something solid that I am proud of. I wouldn't have been able to get to where I am today without the love and the support of all of the wonderful people in my life.

Thank you first to my family, both blood and found, who have loved me unconditionally and supported me always. Thank you to my parents, my dog, and my best friend who at this point is basically my sister and has been right beside me figuring out all this craziness with me, Lily Darling. Your words of encouragement and feedback has always, and will continue to, mean the world to me.

Thank you to my various editors, Davida Smith-Keita, Kristy Carter, and Tracy Seybold and those early readers who gave my feedback including my parents, Cora Sangree and Teresa Calabrese, and others including Olivia Jane Smith, Darryl Alladice, and Joy Rosenthal.

Finally, thank you to everyone who: gave me their time for a personal interview, pre-ordered the eBook, paperback, and multiple copies to make publishing possible, helped spread the word about *All the Little Things*, and helped me publish a book I am proud of. I am completely and sincerely grateful for all of your help and support. Thank you all.

Abigail Vaughn	Becky Marcus
Adam Segal-Isaacson	Belinda Annis
Aja Yamagata-Vance	Benjamin Barner
Alev Sibel Yorulmaz	Beth Sangree
Amy Brown	Bonnie Breen
Amy Goldstein	Bruce Shaw
Amy Sumner	Charles C. Chester
Ann Buttrick	Cora Sangree*
Anna Allanbrook	Dan Perlman~
Annie Grimley	David Gentile
Anthony Calabrese	Dawn Kelly
Antoinette Byam	Diana Calabrese
Barbara Calabrese Stagnitta	Diane Castelucci
Barbara Taragan	Diana Mendez

Diana Greiner*

Elissa Eisenberg

Eric Koester

Ezra Gershman

Frances Ward

Gabriella Belfiglio

Geraldine E. Slaughter

Helen Tocci

Holly Russo

Ilse Sangree

Ivy Trocco

Jack Calabrese

James Calabrese

James Anderson

Janet Shaw Smith

Jaqueline Woodson

Jennifer Croke

Jessica Berenblum

Jordan Scheiner

Joshua Dylan Hunter

Joy Rosenthal*

Kathleen Offenholley

Katie Ronn

Kori Goldberg

Kristen Kaelin

Lara Helena Kuhn

Lauren Gardner

Laurie Matthews

Linda Darling

Linda Villarosa

Liz Selleck

Luna Toro

Marcie Frishberg

Marguerite Calabrese

Michelle Leimsider

Mira Isreal

Miranda Gavitt

Megan O'Donnell

Mo Rajji Courtney

Michael Shaw

Nancy Langston~

Nancy Salomon

Nancy Soyer*

Norma Lowry

Odette Woitschek

Olivia Jane Smith

Patricia Dungey

Paul Tainsh

Penina Hirshman

Peter Mulroy

Rachael Wilde

Robin Tainsh

Rosanne Calabrese*

Sammi Cohen

Sandra Kuhn

Shari Boiskin

Sonja Hubbert

Stephanie Grant

Stephanie Squire

Susan Westover

Tom Jones

Vibert Parris

William Feerick

William Gibbons

Willow Parchment

Wittika MacKenzie-Chaplet

Yolanda Lowry

Key: *multiple copies/campaign contributions
~Interviewed